BAY
LEXICON

B
A
Y

LEXICON

JANE WOLFF

McGill-Queen's University Press

Montreal & Kingston • London • Chicago

© McGill-Queen's University Press 2021

ISBN 978-0-2280-0685-5 (paper)
ISBN 978-0-2280-0791-3 (ePDF)

Legal deposit third quarter 2021
Bibliothèque nationale du Québec

Printed in Canada on acid-free paper that is 100% ancient forest
free (100% post-consumer recycled), processed chlorine free

This book has been published with the help of a grant from the
Canadian Federation for the Humanities and Social Sciences,
through the Awards to Scholarly Publications Program, using
funds provided by the Social Sciences and Humanities Research
Council of Canada.

Funded by the   Financé par le
Government   gouvernement
of Canada   du Canada

Canada

Canada Council   Conseil des arts
for the Arts   du Canada

We acknowledge the support of the Canada Council for the Arts.

Nous remercions le Conseil des arts du Canada de son soutien.

Library and Archives Canada Cataloguing in Publication

Title: Bay lexicon / Jane Wolff.
Names: Wolff, Jane, author.
Description: Includes bibliographical references and index.
Identifiers: Canadiana (print) 20210169338 | Canadiana (ebook)
   20210169516 | ISBN 9780228006855 (paper) | ISBN
   9780228007913 (ePDF)
Subjects: LCSH: Shorelines—California—San Francisco Bay. |
   LCSH: Landscapes—California—San Francisco Bay. | LCSH: San
   Francisco Bay (Calif.)—Environmental conditions. | LCSH: San
   Francisco Bay (Calif.)—Geography.
Classification: LCC F868.S156 W65 2021 | DDC 979.4/61—dc23

I wish to acknowledge that the land this book discusses is the traditional territory of the Ohlone people. I remember their continued connection to this region and give thanks to them for allowing me to live, work, and learn on their traditional homeland. I offer respect to their Elders and to all Ohlone people of the past and present.

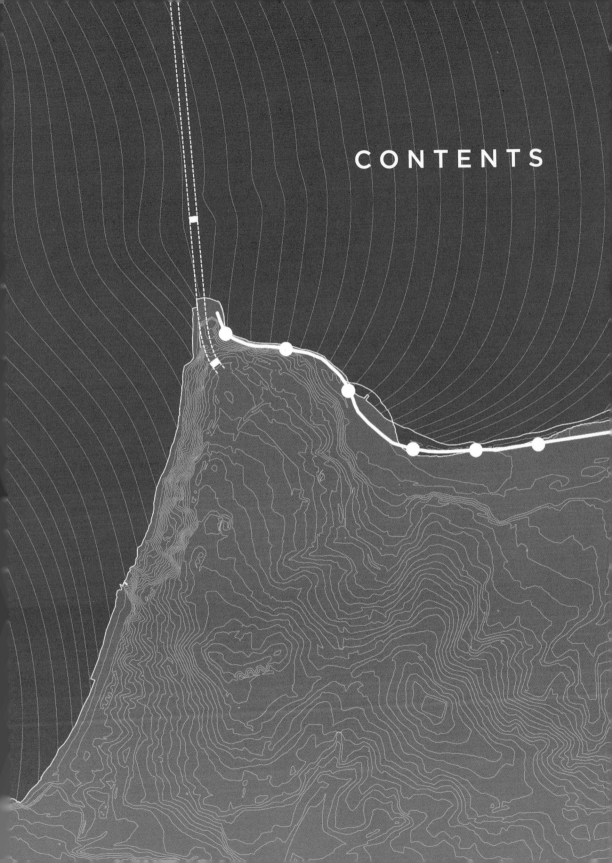

CONTENTS

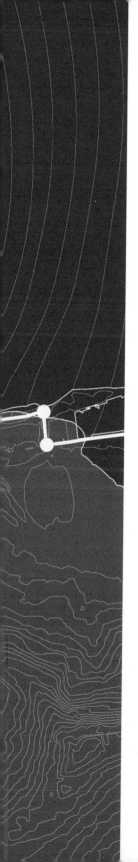

BAY

LEXICON

Introduction

Why a Lexicon?

I grew up with a beautiful story about the ties between vocabulary and acuity: it said that the Inuit had twenty-seven words for snow and that the nuances of their lexicon allowed them to see differences the rest of us missed. That story, which still circulates in arenas ranging from kindergartens to the *Washington Post* (the tallies vary), emerged from Franz Boas's early twentieth-century study of the relationships between culture and language.[1] It was taken up by his followers Edward Sapir and Benjamin Whorf, who contended that language simultaneously shapes and mirrors our perceptions of what's around us.[2] It's useful today as a cautionary tale in a moment of environmental crisis, when the places that most of us know test – and defy – the vocabulary we've inherited for describing landscapes.

The English language tends to separate what's human from what's not, but the age of the Anthropocene[3] blurs that boundary. Human actions intersect with environmental processes everywhere, from the densest cities to the wildest conservation areas. The reciprocal, reiterative, cumulative exchanges between people and the rest of the world have given rise to places where it is no longer possible to draw lines between nature and culture, between economy and ecology, and sometimes even between categories that seem as clear as land and water. To call such divides a product of our collective imagination is not

---

1 Franz Boas, *Handbook of American Indian Languages*, 25. A century after Boas's book, Scott Heyes's "Between the Trees and the Tides: Inuit Ways of Discriminating Space in a Coastal and Boreal Landscape" documented the Kangiqsualujjuaq Inuits' rich and varied vocabulary for littoral landscape features that would be indistinguishable to outsiders.

2 In his 1940 essay "Science and Linguistics," Whorf wrote, "We dissect nature along lines laid down by our native languages. The categories and types that we isolate from the world of phenomena we do not find there because they stare every observer in the face; on the contrary, the world is presented in a kaleidoscopic flux of impressions which has to be organized by our minds – and this means largely by the linguistic systems in our minds."

3 To make the point that human activities have profoundly transformed all of Earth's ecological systems, atmospheric chemist Paul J. Crutzen defined the Anthropocene as a new geological epoch "supplementing the Holocene – the warm period of the past 10–12 millennia. The Anthropocene could be said to have started in the latter part of the eighteenth century when analyses of air trapped in polar ice showed the beginning of growing global concentrations of carbon dioxide and methane. This date also happens to coincide with James Watt's design of the steam engine in 1784." He introduced the term in his paper "Geology of Mankind" in *Nature* 415 (2002): 23.

to deny that there are forces properly categorized as human and forces over which people have no control. It's to say that the landscapes we know today are hybrids. Streets break city grids to follow the paths of buried creeks. Terraces render steep slopes as staggered planes. Piers make homes for barnacles and starfish. Pavements warp as trees grow. Because they're mixed in character, these places are hard to describe; because language is intimately tied to perception, their nuances are hidden in plain sight.

The costs of the gap between language and landscape are high. Since 2005, North America has seen a string of calamities from Hurricane Katrina and Superstorm Sandy to floods that swamped Calgary, Houston, Winnipeg, and Toronto. These events were no surprise to landscape scholars and ecologists: the havoc they wrought was the predictable outcome of back-and-forth interactions between dynamic environments and engineering interventions made to permit their intense use. Time after time, though, the general public didn't register that pattern. Debate raged about whether the catastrophes were natural disasters or engineering failures when the correct answer was both, or neither. Not many people had the ability to read the landscape, to translate its physical circumstances into representational terms that could explain what had happened or suggest how to move forward more sustainably.

The dilemmas caused by language gaps are not confined to the aftermath of emergency. Even in places where calamity has not yet hit, climate change, sea level rise, sprawling urbanization, and out-of-date infrastructure have set the stage for trouble. And though they're bombarded by news about environmental crisis, most people don't have an adequate vocabulary to characterize the essential qualities of the places where they live or discuss the possibilities that lie ahead. The lack of nuanced, commonly understood language limits public discussion, and that makes effective agency difficult for technical experts, policy-makers, politicians, and citizens – for anyone with a stake in the future. Whatever our roles in transforming the landscape, our actions depend on what we argue for, and our arguments for change emerge from our ways of describing the places we know now. Vocabulary shapes the way we see the world: its power as a lens turns the compilation of a landscape lexicon into a reckoning with hybrid ecologies.

A Test Case: Vocabulary for San Francisco Bay

In its reckoning with San Francisco's shoreline, *Bay Lexicon* owes debts to a number of beautiful books about language and landscape. Some, directed in the main toward expert audiences, examine and decipher physical patterns in the environment; others, intended for a wider circle of readers, investigate the meanings of words connected to places.[4] *Bay Lexicon* is a hybrid: it documents the material landscape to generate words and images that can be shared across different points of view. Its ambition is to offer people a way to talk to one another. Conceived as a case study, this book examines a particular site in order to propose methods for observing, documenting, and reconsidering the complex circumstances that emerge in so many intensely inhabited places. The terms laid out here are designed to be translated, adapted, and used far beyond San Francisco Bay.

The edge of the bay makes a useful test case for several reasons. It's a compelling place, and identifying, describing, and investigating the characteristics of hybrid ecologies in such a vibrant setting can help distill broadly applicable questions for use in more muted situations. And it embodies forces and tendencies that have shaped urban waterfronts across the continent. San Francisco, like many significant North American cities, owes its existence to its favorable location on the shore. San Francisco Bay was an essential point of connection between the Pacific Ocean and the interior of the continent, and the city grew up beside a sheltered cove that offered safe anchorage and proximity to deep water. From its origins as a colonial military outpost, San Francisco became a trading and banking center where raw materials and finished goods were exchanged and money was concentrated. With container shipping and globalization, the region's main port moved to the other side of the bay, and the city's industrial economy was replaced by technology and tourism. The edge of San Francisco Bay represents a landscape type. If you come from someplace else, you might not recognize the details, but the big themes will likely be familiar.

Variations on the history, current circumstances, and possible future of San Francisco's shoreline appear all over the developed world, from New York, Boston, Toronto, Vancouver, and Houston to London and Rotterdam. Different as they are, these waterfronts have had comparable trajectories. They were constructed with earthworks that transformed ambiguous edges along oceans, lakes, estuaries, or rivers into working harbors. Their ports, built for sailing ships, grew and changed with advances in marine technology between the middle of the nineteenth century and the second part of the twentieth. Their cities became centers for financial, commercial, and industrial enterprises that supported and profited from port activity.

---

4   The first category includes Ian McHarg's *Design with Nature*, Christopher Alexander and colleagues' *A Pattern Language*, Anne Whiston Spirn's *Granite Garden* and *Language of Landscape*, and William Morrish's *Civilizing Terrains*. The second group includes John Stilgoe's *Shallow Water Dictionary* and *What Is Landscape?*; Barry Lopez and Debra Gwartney's *Home Ground*; Stephan Harrison, Steve Pile, and Nigel Thrift's *Patterned Ground*; Robert Macfarlane's *Landmarks*; and Robert Macfarlane and Jackie Morris's *Lost Words*. These last two were recent bestsellers.

Over the past fifty years, industry has left these cities for cheaper labor markets in the developing world. Shipping has moved from old wharves to new facilities that can accommodate giant container vessels and the staging areas required to transfer containers from sea to land transport. Obsolete port lands have fallen out of use and, often, into dereliction. Since the turn of the twenty-first century, economies are shifting from labor to leisure, and urban waterfronts across North America and Europe have been recast as pleasure grounds. The timing is ironic: the realization that the shoreline is an amenity is giving rise to a renaissance just as the threat of sea level rise is making itself felt.

Today these waterfronts, all of them built up and out from marshy ground and tidelands, lie at the front line of flooding. The climate emergency means that urban coastlines all over the developed world will need to be reimagined. The transformation won't be simple. Substantial changes will demand widespread political support, and these places demonstrate a degree of hybridity that most people don't have the vocabulary to recognize or discuss. The Anthropocene has made building landscape literacy an urgent task.[5]

The edge of San Francisco demonstrates this problem vividly. Most people love the landscape better than they understand it: San Francisco Bay's power as scenery has obscured its ecological complexity, its natural and cultural dynamics, and its ongoing evolution as a metropolitan centerpiece. Not everyone knows that the bay belongs to two watersheds. One, visible from the shoreline, is defined by the low mountains of the Coast Ranges. The other, too distant to see, extends to the Sierra Nevada, the Cascades, and the

At the scale of the city, San Francisco Bay is defined by the shoreline.

Credit: These maps were created using ArcGIS® software by Esri. ArcGIS® and ArcMap™ are the intellectual property of Esri and are used herein under license. Copyright © Esri. All rights reserved. For more information about Esri® software, please visit www.esri.com.
Alameda County Information Technology Department, "Alameda County Street Centerlines" [Feature Layer], *Alameda County Open Data*; City and County of San Francisco, "SF Shoreline and Islands" [shapefile], *DataSF*; City and County of San Francisco, "Streets – Active and Retired" [shapefile]. *DataSF*; County of Marin, "Marin County Boundary" [shapefile], *Marin County Open Data*; Esri, "Marin County Roads" [Feature Layer]; Esri, GEBCO, NOAA, *National Geographic*, DeLorme, HERE, Geonames.org, and other contributors, "Ocean" [basemap]; Esri, HERE, Garmin, INCREMENT P, © OpenStreetMap contributors, and the GIS user community. "World Dark Grey" [basemap]; Esri, Airbus DS, USGS, NGA, NASA, CGIAR, N Robinson, NCEAS, NLS, OS, NMA, Geodatastyrelsen, Rijkswaterstaat, GSA, Geoland, FEMA, Intermap, and the GIS user community, "World Hillshade" [basemap].

---

5 Anne Whiston Spirn's work with community members in West Philadelphia, detailed in her essay "Landscape Literacy and Design for Ecological Democracy," demonstrates the political and social power of public knowledge about hybrid landscapes.

0   1   2mi

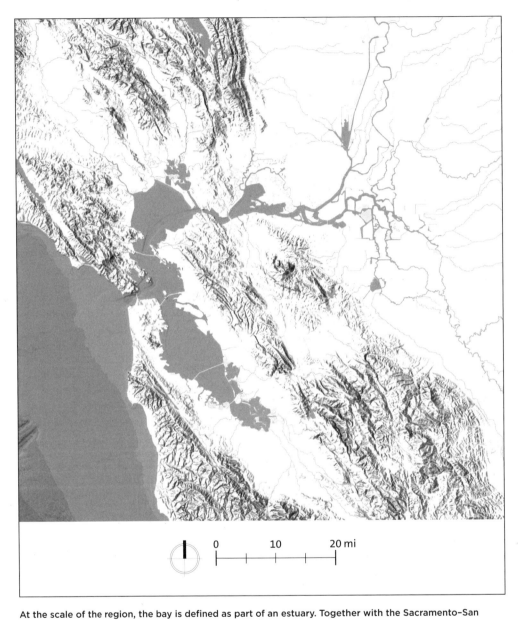

0   10   20 mi

At the scale of the region, the bay is defined as part of an estuary. Together with the Sacramento–San Joaquin Delta, it connects California's great interior rivers to the Pacific Ocean.

Credit: California Department of Fish and Wildlife, "California Streams" [shapefile], *California Open Data Portal*; Esri, GEBCO, NOAA, *National Geographic*, DeLorme, HERE, Geonames.org, and other contributors, "Ocean" [basemap]; Esri, HERE, Garmin, INCREMENT P, © OpenStreetMap contributors, and the GIS user community, "World Dark Grey" [basemap]; Esri, Airbus DS, USGS, NGA, NASA, CGIAR, N Robinson, NCEAS, NLS, OS, NMA, Geodatastyrelsen, Rijkswaterstaat, GSA, Geoland, FEMA, Intermap, and the GIS user community, "World Hillshade" [basemap].

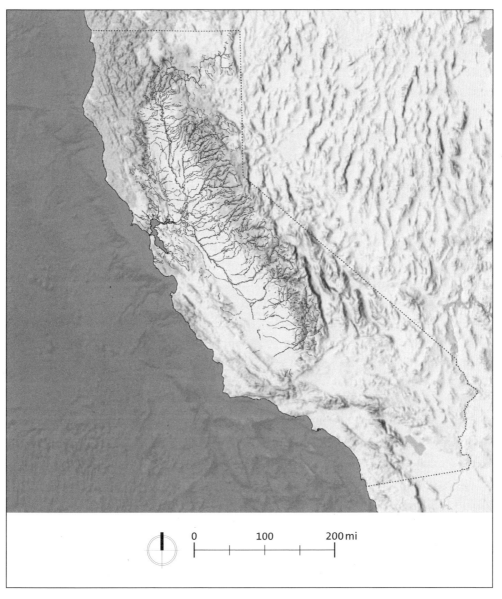

At the scale of the watershed, the bay is defined by all the water that flows into it from California's coastal and interior mountain ranges.

Credit: California Department of Fish and Wildlife, "California Streams" [shapefile], *California Open Data Portal*; Esri, GEBCO, NOAA, *National Geographic*, DeLorme, HERE, Geonames.org, and other contributors, "Ocean" [basemap]; Esri, HERE, Garmin, INCREMENT P, © OpenStreetMap contributors, and the GIS user community. "World Dark Grey" [basemap]; Esri, Airbus DS, USGS, NGA, NASA, CGIAR, N Robinson, NCEAS, NLS, OS, NMA, Geodatastyrelsen, Rijkswaterstaat, GSA, Geoland, FEMA, Intermap, and the GIS user community. "World Hillshade" [basemap]; State of California Department of Technology, "CA USGS Watershed Boundary Dataset (12-Digit Hydrologic Units)" [shapefile]. *California Open Data Portal*.

Tulare Basin. The last segment of the largest tidal estuary on the west coast of the Americas, San Francisco Bay is the Great Central Valley's only outlet to the Pacific. The access it provided to California's interior meant it would be an important landscape economically as well as ecologically, and its harbor was the first engine for growth in San Francisco. Since the arrival of European settlers in the eighteenth century, the bay and its edges have been shaped by unromantic agendas: military strategy, resource extraction, commerce, real estate speculation, industry, and politics. Those endeavors arose (and remain) in constant dialogue with living systems and environmental forces at scales from the microscopic to the regional, and beyond.

In the middle of the nineteenth century, California's Gold Rush made San Francisco Bay the most valuable port in the United States. Today the bay lies at the center of an urban agglomeration that stretches across nine counties. The landscapes at its edge are intensively used, and sea level rise will create acute pressure for change. Public discussion about what to do is in its early stages. Research groups at universities and think tanks have begun to propose new kinds of physical and social infrastructure. Ideas range from floating houses and elevated roadways to systems of government that replace cities and counties with jurisdictions defined by geographical and hydrological boundaries.[6] Working toward resilience won't be simple. Negotiating the future will demand a shared vocabulary that helps people see what goes on behind and beyond the bay's iconic image. *Bay Lexicon* aims to meet that need. It defines working language for the hybrid landscape of San Francisco Bay through two methods: first, the observation, documentation, and analysis of places and phenomena a person can see as she walks along the shore, and second, the thematic classification of those places and phenomena.

---

6 Proposals for responding to sea level rise in the Bay Area have emerged from research institutions, advocacy groups, and government organizations. These efforts include "Resilient by Design: Bay Area Challenge," a design competition for sites around San Francisco Bay; "Operational Landscape Units for San Francisco Bay," a project that seeks to address climate change within geographic rather than political boundaries; the *SFEI San Francisco Bay Resilience Atlas,* which makes scientific information available to diverse audiences; "Baylands Ecosystem Habitat Goals Project," which works to restore tidelands; "Resilient Infrastructure as Seas Rise (RISeR) SF Bay," a research project of the University of California's Climate Readiness Institute; and "Artistic Practice towards Urban Resilience (APUR)," a collaboration between the Exploratorium and the University of California's Department of Civil and Environmental Engineering.

Lexicon as Tool

Bay Lexicon considers circumstances and situations that exist below the surface of popular consciousness. It investigates ways in which the tangible landscape expresses complicated relationships between natural forces and cultural intentions. It offers verbal and visual language in the service of related causes: perception, the awareness of what's around us; observation, the act of careful watching; understanding, the recognition of significance; and speculation, the contemplation of possibility. It brings together different kinds of information, at different scales, from different fields of expertise and points of view. Its plural methods make it a tool with plural uses: as a technical document that examines how things work, a historical document that looks at how the landscape evolved (and is still evolving), a cultural document that brings values to light, and a political document that frames discussion about how and why the landscape might respond to the pressures acting on it today.[7]

A last note about origins and ambitions: *Bay Lexicon* was conceived and executed over the course of a ten-year collaboration with the Exploratorium, a San Francisco museum that has long made specialized content about the basic sciences available to people who aren't scientists. Particle physicist Frank Oppenheimer founded the museum in 1969 to address the widening gap he perceived between the social and political power of science and technology and the lives of ordinary citizens.[8] Since its inception, the Exploratorium has used art to frame and stimulate its visitors' perception and understanding of scientific phenomena. This book emerged from an initiative to extend Oppenheimer's ideas and values into the arena of the environment.[9] It might be characterized as a translation project: it puts varied, complicated content into language that cuts across disciplinary boundaries and levels of expertise. The goal is to provide synthetic, rigorous information essential for thoughtful discussion about the landscape's future to the range of people who should have a say.

---

7 This book builds on ideas explored in my museum installation "Bay Lexicon," the accompanying gallery broadside "Bay Lexicon: Vocabulary as Manifesto," and essays "Lexicon as Theory" and "City, Nature, Infrastructure: A Brief Lexicon."

8 Oppenheimer, "A Rationale for a Science Museum," 206. Oppenheimer's own experience offered a clear view of this gap. He began his career in high-level physics research with the Manhattan Project and at the University of Minnesota; after Joseph McCarthy added him to his blacklist, he worked as a rancher and high-school science teacher.

9 This effort, initiated by Peter Richards and Susan Schwartzenberg as a study of the invisible dynamics of San Francisco Bay, grew into content for an entirely new gallery when the museum moved to San Francisco's Piers 15 and 17. In 2007, my artist's residency produced ideas for an observatory gallery with a lexicon at its center; Ms Schwartzenberg curated the Bay Observatory and commissioned my permanent installation, "Bay Lexicon." Since then, the Observatory has become a nexus for public discussion about sea level rise in the Bay Area.

Keywords

Bay Lexicon's keywords address the problem of imprecise language in hybrid landscapes. They consider generic words in the specific context of San Francisco Bay, and they shed light on differences that everyday definitions obscure. In ordinary use, the word *land* doesn't distinguish the unstable ground of San Francisco's constructed edge from the solid bedrock of its hills, even though the conditions of their inhabitation are not at all alike; *water* lumps together what comes from the ocean, the rivers, and the sky despite chemical variations that have profound implications for living beings.

Keys open locks, and keywords unlock meaning. In libraries and databases, they're search terms for finding material that speaks to a common topic. In cryptography, they crack codes and ciphers. In *Bay Lexicon*, keywords articulate a set of themes that underlie and organize San Francisco's shoreline: they provide a vocabulary to decipher the landscape.

The keywords that follow have a reiterative relationship to the field guide in the second half of the book. They were distilled from concrete observations made along the waterfront and documented one by one in the field guide's entries. Each keyword is defined through the examination of entries whose content speaks to the same topic in varied ways, and the meanings that accrue reveal relationships among places, processes, moments, and stories that might not seem to be connected.

The keywords comprise six categories of thought and activity related to the intense inhabitation of a landscape:

- the classification of territory and terrain (land, water)
- the study of the natural world (physics, chemistry, biology)
- the exploitation of resources (defense, commerce)
- the domestication of the environment (navigation, construction, infrastructure)
- the practices of everyday life (work, play)
- the registration of time (interval, souvenir)

Most field entries participate in the definition of more than one keyword (for instance, information from the entry about ships' pilots appears under *infrastructure, navigation, physics,* and *work*). Each keyword points to a different aspect of the field entry's content and situates it differently in relation to other entries.

Bay Lexicon's keywords take on meaning place by place and instance by instance. They reveal ways in which the material world gives form to abstract ideas, and they offer a framework for classifying and reclassifying observations of the landscape. As they construct relationships between and among bounded sites and broad ideas, they lay out a method for developing language calibrated to the nuances of the shoreline. They are a case study in using the particulars of a landscape to re-examine words that are usually taken for granted.

This vocabulary is offered as a model, not a template. The same keywords might not apply to every place, and even if they do, their definitions will vary in different locales. What matters most is specificity, nuance, and clarity. The power of keywords lies in their ability to speak to (and for) people with different points of view.

Language colors observations in the present and speculations about the future. It's hard to perceive what we can't name, and our ideas about what's possible emerge from our perceptions of what already exists. Because words used generically hide complexity, they limit imagination. Keywords that illuminate the tangled character of hybrid land-scapes offer better means to discuss the status quo – and to advocate for change.

Keywords 1
Territory and Terrain

Deciphering the edge of San Francisco Bay begins with observing difference in the landscape. Standing on the shoreline – or looking at a map – you might be struck first by the contrast between land and water. They look like opposites. Land is dry, and water is wet. Land is fixed, and water moves. Land can be inhabited, and water can't, or at least, not without boats. Everyday language describes land and water as discrete, finite entities: the bay is a body of water that touches a mass of land. The *Oxford English Dictionary* uses one to define the other. It says that land is "the solid portion of the earth's surface, as opposed to … *water*."[1] So do most maps. The flat blue plane of San Francisco Bay begins where land ends.

A closer look at the edge of the bay suggests that land and water have plural definitions and ambiguous borders.[2] Neither kind of territory is homogeneous; each includes a range of different material conditions with their own origins, properties, and possibilities. And whatever dictionaries and maps say, the lines between land and water are neither definite nor constant. They vary from hour to hour with the tides. They've shifted with the advances and retreats of ice sheets and glaciers. They've moved because of people's ways of living in the landscape. They're changing again, right now and before our eyes, as sea level rise calls the boundaries of the recent past into question.

Land

Reference dictionaries agree that land means solid ground,[3] something fixed, stable, inhabitable and, in the United States, ownable. San Francisco's edge undermines that certainty. The land along the shore looks like a consistent surface, but it varies in its source,

---

1 *Oxford English Dictionary*, s.v. "Land."
2 Anuradha Mathur and Dilip da Cunha have written about this ambiguity at length, most recently in their essay "Wetness Is Everywhere."
3 This definition and the keyword definitions that follow are distilled from several sources, including the *Oxford English Dictionary*, the *American Heritage Dictionary of the English Language*, and Google definitions, which are based on the *Oxford Pocket English Dictionary*.

its composition, its character, and its capacity. Sailing charts from the eighteenth and early nineteenth centuries distinguished between *terra firma* and the uncertain terrain of tidelands and marshlands that lay between solid ground and open water. Transformed in the wake of the Gold Rush, those ambiguous places were made into a new kind of land whose construction belonged part and parcel to the building of the city.

Collective memories are strangely short. Walking along the shoreline, it's hard to imagine that the conditions underfoot haven't always existed or that they won't persist. But thinking about the future means remembering that the land at the edge of the bay is dynamic. Since San Francisco's beginnings, it has changed with people's interpretation of the landscape's meaning, and changes in interpretation have given rise to changes in inhabitation.

What sailing charts showed as *terra firma* was old land, formed three or four million years ago when the movement of tectonic plates pushed seafloor sediment up into crumpled folds.[4] Two hundred fifty years ago, when the first Europeans arrived at the entrance to San Francisco Bay, they read those folds as the bedrock hills of the Coast Range. Spanish colonizers recognized value in the high, solid terrain above the bay. The hills were places to defend claims to territory. The promontory on the southern side of the Golden Gate became a fort: the Presidio of the Spanish and the Mexicans, then Fort Point when the Americans took California. Control of the old land of the hills meant control of the bay, its harbor, the city that grew up beside it, the rivers that led inland, and the resources that lay upstream. The discovery of gold in the Sierra Nevada raised the stakes. San Francisco Bay was the best route to the mines.

The same qualities that made the hills into lookouts for people who wanted to control access to the bay turned them into landmarks for people trying to find their way in. The first Spanish accounts of San Francisco Bay named the hill on the northeastern corner of San Francisco Loma Alta – High Hill – and the name gave it meaning for travelers who followed. Inhabited, the landmark became a vantage point. Its height gave people the chance to see over a great distance, and that vista – or prospect – earned it another name: an American settler's sketch called it "Prospect Hill."[5] Because it offered views to and from the Golden Gate and the harbor, the vantage point became a signaling site: Telegraph Hill. In 1908, the hill's west side greeted Theodore Roosevelt's Great White Fleet with a sign that read "WELCOME."

By that time, the east face of the hill had changed substantially because of a second interpretation of its value: as a source of rock. Telegraph Hill was quarried for ships' ballast

---

4 Elder, "Geology of the Golden Gate Headlands."
5 Myrick, *San Francisco's Telegraph Hill*, 16.

and then for stone to fill marshes and mudflats beside the harbor. Quarrying created deep cracks in the hill. Houses on the surface collapsed into fissures, and the east slope was carved back to a precarious, almost vertical cliff. Land solid enough to have lasted for millions of years was rendered impermanent and unstable in a few decades. The old land of the hill became a contradiction. Its significance as a landmark depended on its fixity, but its worth as raw material turned it into something malleable.

The rock pulled from Telegraph Hill was reassembled to make new land at the shore. Until the middle of the nineteenth century, the dry land of the Coast Range met the open water of the bay along a margin of tidelands. Twice a day, at low and high tides, the tidelands came to light and disappeared. They were too shallow to land a boat; they were too wet to build on; and they were too ambiguous to own, at least until federal and state legislation made them available if they were raised above the level of high water.

Piled with rock and rubble, the tidelands looked like solid ground. The new land had a limit, a seawall whose top was higher than high tide and whose foundation rested on rock below the muddy, sandy bay floor. Over fifty years, people pumped away the water on the landward side of the wall and filled in the space that was left. New land covered shallow coves where streams met the bay; in some places, it swallowed offshore rocks, fragments of old land that poked above the water. It buried the old, scalloped, uncertain zone between land and water beneath a single plane and behind a definite line.

Easier to occupy than the steep slopes of the hills, the new land provided space to build a working city. Its construction gave businesses, warehouses, and factories easy access to deepwater wharves. Over time, it has supported denser and denser inhabitation. The city's endless demand for inhabitable space has produced vertical extensions of the ground: high-rises multiply the surface with every story. Everything seems solid enough, but appearance belies the reality of the new land's liminal physical state. Height at the water's edge requires footings deep enough to reach the old land under fill and mud. The foundations of the Embarcadero Center's twenty-, thirty-, and forty-five-story towers had to be dug sixteen stories deep in order to rest on bedrock. From time to time, the tectonic plates that formed San Francisco's old land shift again, and the earthquakes that ensue remind everyone that new land is shaky ground. Between earthquakes, the US Geological and Geodetic Survey's maps of liquefaction risk serve as reminders of the ambiguous territory on early sailing charts of the bay. Those maps' hazard zones track the boundaries of land constructed since the Gold Rush.

New or old, land transcends and upends people's plans and desires. Even the solid rock of Telegraph Hill fractured when it was mined, and sea level rise will reveal the impermanence of a century and a half's worth of fill. Notwithstanding all the maps that show water as a bounded field, higher tides will reclaim the territory along the shore. Water will redefine what we know as land.

Water

The monochromatic definition of water on most maps is matched by what's in standard dictionaries: water is colorless, odorless, transparent, two parts hydrogen to one part oxygen, usually encountered as a liquid, falls as rain, and makes up rivers, lakes, and seas. But the water at the edge of the bay is neither neutral nor undifferentiated. Its characteristics vary with its origins: some of it comes from the ocean, some from the rivers and streams that drain local hills and distant mountains. It moves constantly. It changes with wind, tides, and rain. It has agency. It shapes land, and it shapes possibilities for all living creatures: plants, animals, and people. Sometimes people put water to work; other times they're subject to its power.

People who watch the bay know that water changes the landscape every day. Rising and falling with the flow and ebb of the tides, it lifts all boats (or lets them down); it marks the face of the seawall and moves in and out of remnant streams and marshes. Water's rise and fall has changed the shore of San Francisco Bay every day, every month, and every season for ten thousand years, since the last Ice Age ended. The bay didn't exist until then. Its antecedents were a valley that ran north and south through the Coast Range and an ancient river that collected water from the Sierra Nevada mountains and Tulare Lake. The river ran from east to west across the valley. It carved a deep channel between what's now the Carquinez Strait and what's now the Golden Gate, and then it flowed twenty-five miles over a shallow plain to the coast. When the vast ice sheets of the Pleistocene Epoch melted, the water they released raised the level of the seas. The coast moved inland; the ocean came through the Golden Gate and flooded the valley; and the ancient river was drowned. Rising water turned the valley into a bay, and it made isolated hills at the center of the valley into islands: Angel Island, Alcatraz, Yerba Buena.

Geologically, the islands in the bay still belong to the hills of the Coast Range. Linguistically, they've been reclassified. Islands are defined in opposition to the mainland; they're understood as places of discontinuity, separation, and solitude. The Americans who built San Francisco made use of the distance created by water. Angel Island and Alcatraz became sites of exile. For decades they housed people who had been banished from everyday life – prisoners – or people who were being denied entry – immigrants. Now they're voluntary destinations, refuges for people to flee the confines of the city, at least temporarily.

Treasure Island was made for escape: it provided space for the fantastic constructions of the 1939 World's Fair. People built the island because water had failed to define land clearly. When the bay formed, the lower reaches of Yerba Buena Island were barely submerged. What had been land turned into shoals. The shoals created a hazard for ships, but in the 1930s, the New Deal's public works programs turned something dangerous into something useful. Piled with rock and rubble, the shoals – land just under water – became an island – land surrounded by water. Ground gained in any ongoing exchange is subject to loss. As sea level rises, water may well cover the island again.

Wherever the shoreline, water moving along the coast changes the land it touches. Set into motion by currents, tides, waves, and storms, water has the energy to carry sand and sediment from one place to another. It keeps the shoreline in a constant state of migration: longshore drift. As waves break and retreat, they move sediment down the coast. When the waves meet an obstacle, like the abandoned jetty at Heron's Head, they drop sediment; over time, water builds land.

Water moves land across watersheds, too. Some of the sediment in San Francisco Bay comes from upstream. Rivers have brought it there from the Sierra Nevada mountains. Set into motion by the force of gravity, water moving down steep slopes picks up particles of weathering rock. Twenty-six rivers run toward the bay from the western slope of the Sierra Nevada range. They cross the Great Central Valley, come together in the California Delta, and flow through the Carquinez Strait. Then water that's traveled from the mountains spreads out into the bay, and the fragments of earth it has carried fall to the bottom until currents and waves pick them up again.

The ability of water to move land made it a tool for the mining of the Sierra Nevada. Hydraulics turned water into an agent of abrasion, extraction, and destruction. Shot through hoses and nozzles under high pressure, it blasted tons and tons of rock, gravel, and sediment from the mountains. Outwash carried the detritus all the way to San Francisco Bay – including mercury that had been used to separate gold from ore. The mercury keeps traveling: it goes from water into the food web and returns to land when terrestrial creatures (like people) eat what they pull from the bay. A century and a half after hydraulic mining was banned, the watershed contains enough mercury to contaminate the bay for ten millennia.[6] Running from the mountains to the shore, rivers carry a connection from the present to the past – and to the future.

---

6 Hydraulic mining was prohibited by the court ruling *Edwards Woodruff v. North Bloomfield Gravel Mining Company*, 18 F. 753 (9th Cir. 1884).

Water flows from the mountains to the bay and from the bay to the ocean. San Francisco Bay is the last chamber of an estuary[7] where the rivers of the Sierra Nevada and the Central Valley meet the Pacific. They meet, but they don't merge; the plume of the rivers floats above a wedge of the sea. The salt wedge moves inland when tides flow from the ocean and seaward when they ebb, or when rain and melting snow send more fresh water down from the mountains. The ocean's pulse is most powerful between the Golden Gate and the Carquinez Strait. In the southern part of the bay, beyond the direct exchange between the Sierras and the Pacific, salt and fresh water meet at local scales. Estuaries form at the mouths of creeks flowing from the Coast Range hills and at the sewer outlets of nearby towns. The water's changing saltiness tracks the dynamics of the bay's watersheds, large and small.

San Francisco owes its existence to water. It became an important place because San Francisco Bay linked the ocean to the rivers of California's interior. The water of the bay lies at the center of the metropolitan landscape in every way but one: even when the flows from upstream are greatest, it's too salty to drink. Since the 1930s, the people who live at the edge of the bay have been using water brought from across the watershed by a route separated from the rivers: an aqueduct. High in the Sierra Nevada, fifteen miles north of Yosemite, a dam across the Hetch Hetchy valley captures a third of the Tuolumne River.[8] Water leaves this granite reservoir through tunnels and pipes; it crosses the watershed unseen and emerges from taps across the city as if by magic. That flow sustains more than two million human lives,[9] but many of the people who drink it don't know its source – or its relationship to the water they see from the shore.

The aqueduct is not the only place where water is hidden. People don't see the water that moves constantly through the land beneath their feet. Rain used to feed streams that ran overland to the bay, but cities are designed to stay dry. Waterproof roofs and roads shed rain into gutters, drains, pipes, and sewers that carry water to the bay as quickly as possible. Public works send urban rivers underground. The roads that wind through the

---

7 San Francisco Bay belongs to the San Francisco Bay-Delta Estuary, the largest tidal estuary on the west coast of the Americas.

8 The dam across Hetch Hetchy was controversial from the beginning. John Muir first described the valley's extraordinary landscape in an 1873 newspaper article; in his book *The Yosemite*, he spoke out against the construction of the reservoir, not least because Hetch Hetchy lay within the boundaries of Yosemite National Park.

9 The San Francisco Public Utility District's Hetch Hetchy reservoir and aqueduct supply water to approximately 85 percent of the agency's 2.7 million residential, commercial, and industrial customers in San Francisco, Alameda, San Mateo, and Santa Clara counties. For further information, see the website of the San Francisco Public Utilities Commission.

city's canyons and valleys cover watercourses. Streets and boulevards buried Islais Creek, but it still runs beneath the pavement, out of sight and out of mind until it emerges in a narrow channel at the edge of the bay.

Water has almost disappeared from the surface of the city, but it's not entirely contained or tamed. When it drifts over the landscape as fog, it makes edges and outlines indistinct; its slow condensation connects the sky to the ground and leaves everyone (and everything) cool and damp. Rain arrives in larger, faster drops, but when it lands on plants, it, too, falls slowly through their leaves. It sinks into the pores between particles of soil and migrates through those tiny apertures toward the bay. When it descends through terrain remade by retaining walls, their foundations stop its progress. It pools and seeps along the walls. As it moves, it takes soil with it. As soil shifts, the walls begin to crack. The cracks, spread over the whole of hilly San Francisco, serve as reminders that land and water are never truly separate. To observe differences is not to draw absolute boundaries.

Keywords 2
The Natural Sciences

Observing difference in the landscape (the difference between land and water, for instance, or differences within the categories land and water) lies at the foundation of the natural sciences. By studying and classifying the phenomena of the more-than-human environment, science offers explanations of the world as we find it. Most of the people at the edge of the bay aren't scientists, but science builds theories that explain their everyday observations.

The natural sciences divide what's commonly called nature, the world beyond human control, from culture, the products of human thought and effort; science examines artifacts, forces, processes, and phenomena that seem to exist independent of people's intentions, desires, plans, and ambitions. That boundary is artificial. The natural sciences are themselves products of culture: they allow people to explain non-human phenomena to other people. They emerged in specific historical and social contexts, and they're colored by values and beliefs. They're intellectual constructs that describe particular observations as expressions of generalizable hypotheses.

Abstract or concrete, scientific knowledge is intimately connected to tangible processes and experiences at the edge of San Francisco Bay; for instance, sailors reckon constantly with the physical forces that cause tides and waves.[1] And even though physics, chemistry, and biology are defined separately, their subjects come together and overlap in the processes and systems of the bay. They provide different lenses for examining the same environment.

The natural sciences help people understand and represent what they observe and experience. As they shape individual and collective ideas about what's possible or likely, they inform cultural changes to the environment at scales from the front yard to the watershed. Knowing why and how things happen in the landscape's more-than-human systems brings to light possibilities for engaging and changing them. Those engagements (and the unexpected consequences that regularly ensue) serve as reminders that understanding and representing natural systems is not the same as controlling them.

---

1 Richard White, *The Organic Machine*.

Physics

Physics considers the inanimate world in terms of matter (bodies and substances that have mass and take up space) and energy (the capacity of a body or system to produce movement or other physical change). It studies interactions between matter and energy from the smallest possible scales to the largest, from the particles that make up atoms to planets, stars, and galaxies. At those extremes, physical phenomena are abstractions that can't be grasped without high-level math and sophisticated experiments. In between, at the scales of the body and the landscape, interactions between matter and energy work in plain sight to shape the edge of the bay. Physics accounts for the movement of water and for ways in which people can move across the water; it describes the behavior of light and sound; it determines whether people see themselves as shadows or as reflections. Everyday observations of the landscape bring a colloquial understanding of physical phenomena, and that understanding becomes a means for action.

Building San Francisco meant changing the shoreline's relationship to tides; the construction of the seawall and the new, dry ground behind it required the ability to predict high and low water. Tides rise and fall because of gravity, the force that draws objects toward one another, and inertia, the tendency of moving objects to continue in the same direction. Water in oceans (and in the bay) moves with the rotation of the Earth. Inertia would send it flying into space on a tangent, but gravity holds it to the surface of the planet. The balance changes twice a day. The Moon has gravity too, and when it comes closest to the bay, it drags water slightly away from the surface of the Earth: a high tide. Twelve hours later, when the Moon is halfway around the world, inertia gains the upper hand. Water starts to move on a straight-line tangent rather than clinging to the Earth's surface, and the tangent creates a bulge: a second high tide. Low tides happen in between. When the Moon and the Sun line up, their combined gravity tugs on the bay, and high tides are at their highest.

Whether or not they think about gravity and inertia, the pilots who guide ships to and from ports on San Francisco Bay know the tides at every moment of every day. They know waves, too. Waves are not tides. They're products of another physical process, the translation of the wind's energy through water. The wind is itself a translation, an expression of the Sun's energy traveling through air. The Sun heats the Earth unevenly, and where it's warmer, the temperature of the air above the ground increases. Heated, the particles that make up the air gain energy. They expand; the density of the air decreases; the warm air rises; and cooler, denser air takes its place. That movement of air is wind. Wind blowing across a body of water drags the water on the surface forward until its energy is overcome by the force of Earth's gravity. The water falls and pushes what's below it to the surface. Then the process starts over. Each drop of water returns to its starting point. It makes a circle, and together, the circles make a wave that carries energy through the water. A pilot can't move his ship forward with wave energy; he'll just bob up and down.

Though waves don't move water (or boats), they can move land. As they come to the shore, their energy allows water to pick up sand and sediment. A wave breaking at an oblique angle to the coast carries those particles in its direction of travel. As it retreats, the water through which it's moving loses energy. The particles drop, pulled down by Earth's gravity until the next wave carries them farther down the shore. At Heron's Head, a stone jetty extending into the bay intercepts the waves and dampens their energy. The sediment that falls there has built a marsh.

The waves we can touch create waves we can hear. Waves moving across the surface of the bay create echoes that sound through the bathhouse at Aquatic Park. When the waves land, they strike the base of the building, and their energy makes the walls vibrate. The vibration transmits energy to the air, and the energy moves through the air's particles as waves. The waves travel too fast to be felt, but they can be heard: sound waves. The sound waves travel across the room until they hit another wall. Then they bounce back, and we hear them again: an echo. Waves traveling at different speeds make different sounds. On the Golden Gate Bridge, the foghorns on each tower emit waves at different frequencies. Their distinct tones guide ships safely past the bridge. The sounds of the foghorns reach across the city, too. Background music to a foggy day, their waves echo among the hills.

Waves give people not just the sounds of the bay but its sights. Light waves move even faster than sound waves. They express the energy of photons, particles emitted by the Sun (and stars, fires, electrical filaments, and fireflies, among other sources). They travel too fast to be seen, but their behavior becomes evident when they reach boundaries like the one between air and water. When light waves cross from air into clear water, they bend. That bending, or refraction, makes objects seem to bend, too; the vertical pilings under the piers look like they change angles at the surface of the bay. Clouded by suspended sediment, water becomes opaque. The boundary between air and water acts like a projection screen, and people looking down at the bay see the pilings, and themselves, as shadows. When a person looks at the water's surface from certain angles, it acts like a mirror. Light waves graze the bay's edges, strike its surface, and bounce back to her eyes as a reflection. Those waves show her an image of the landscape; if she's standing in the right place, she'll see herself mirrored there, too.

Physical phenomena at the boundary between air and water allow people to perceive the landscape and, sometimes, to notice their own place there. They also let people make use of the landscape. In sailing, they offer opportunities for agency: they let people move across the bay and beyond. When a boat heads downwind, wind pushes its sail forward. Heading upwind works by balancing the pressure of air against a boat's sail with the pressure of water against its keel. The boat heads into the wind at an angle. Its sail curves, and wind action creates a difference in air pressure on each side of the curve. Snapping in to equalize the pressure, the sail tips the boat's hull; the pressure of water against the keel counterbalances the sail; and instead of tipping, the boat moves ahead.

Uphill from the shore, retaining walls also balance forces to prevent tipping. The force of earth pressing against a wall tends to push it outward. Counterbalanced by a foundation broad enough to resist the thrust, retaining walls gain the strength to support building sites: constructed equilibrium. Before there were retaining walls, San Francisco's hills had a different kind of equilibrium. The relationship between gravity (the force pulling matter toward the center of the Earth) and friction (the force that resists motion) created angles of repose: grains of soil and pieces of rock slid downward until they caught against one another and stopped.

Gravity pulls water down hills, too. The faster the water, the more energy it has; the more energy, the greater its ability to overcome the friction that keeps soil in place. The rivers that run down the steep slopes of the Sierra Nevada flow so fast that their energy wears away rock. They carry fragments of the mountains through the Great Central Valley and the California Delta. At the Carquinez Strait, the rivers meet San Francisco Bay. Water spreads out, slows down, loses energy, and drops sediment from the mountains on the bay floor. During the Gold Rush, mining accelerated this process. To get gold from the mountains' centers, miners blasted water from high-pressure hoses against hillsides. That water had so much energy that it turned slopes into gravel. As it flowed into rivers, it had enough energy to carry the gravel to the bay and beyond the Golden Gate. Detritus from hydraulic mines choked streams, raised riverbeds, and piled up on the bottom of the bay. Mercury used to separate gold from ore washed down, too. It's still there. The miners' story is a parable: people who mobilize physical forces can change the landscape forever.

Sometimes people's interventions are only temporary; sometimes they're illusory. The seawall that supports the filled land along San Francisco's shoreline hides the tides, but it doesn't stop them. Pilots know that. At Heron's Head marsh, where the ground slopes down to the water, plants and animals know, too; they thrive in the zone between tides. A person walking there can see water ebb and flow in the channels of the marsh. Even far from shore, someone who watches the night sky can follow the bay's rise and fall. The light of the Moon tells the story. The Moon reflects light from the Sun. When

Earth lies between the Moon and the Sun, all of the light is visible; a full moon means a high tide. When the Moon lies between the Earth and the Sun, none of the light reaches Earth; a new moon means a high tide, too. As weeks and months pass, changing light signals the changing effects of gravity. The forces of physics make the landscape what it is, and they make the landscape legible.

Chemistry

Chemistry studies the characteristics and interactions of different kinds of matter. It classifies substances by the composition and structure of their molecules, and it examines and predicts relationships between molecules of different types. The matter that makes up San Francisco Bay and its watershed varies in space and over time. It changes because of environmental processes and cultural decisions (or accidents). The molecular structures of matter aren't observable at the scale of the body, but the phenomena they create are. A careful observer can see powerful interactions between inanimate substances, and she can register relationships between inanimate substances and the animate world. Variations in the chemistry of the bay and its edges have an impact on what lives there, including people.

The water in the bay all looks the same, but it's not. Most of it comes from the Pacific Ocean; some comes from rivers that drain the Sierra Nevada mountains, the Great Central Valley, and the local hills of the Coast Range; the rest arrives as rain or fog. Ocean water contains dissolved salts. Fresh water doesn't. Though they meet in the bay, chemistry keeps them apart. Salt increases water's mass and density, so fresh water floats above salt water. Their angled boundary changes location with the diurnal and seasonal balance of rivers and tides. The bay's salinity varies from place to place, too; it's saltiest between the Golden Gate and Carquinez Strait. The water's varying salt levels offer habitats to many kinds of plants and animals, but they're too high to maintain healthy human chemistry. To get rid of salt, a person's body draws water from its cells, and its organs fail. Drinking saltwater leads to death by dehydration.

San Francisco's need for potable water led to the construction of the Hetch Hetchy Project. Water that would once have flowed through the Tuolumne River to San Francisco Bay now travels through an aqueduct to the city. Though the dam and reservoir that feed the Hetch Hetchy Aqueduct lie almost two hundred miles upstream from San Francisco Bay, their unintended consequences can be read at the lower end of the watershed. As less fresh water flows from the river, salt water moves farther upstream in the estuary formed by San Francisco Bay and the California Delta, and the change in water chemistry hurts plants and animals accustomed to low salinity. The provision of water to support human life at the estuary's edge has costs for plant and animal life at its center. Massive diversions around and beyond the watershed have multiplied those costs to the point of crisis. For decades, Los Angeles, San Diego, and the irrigated farms of the southern Central Valley have relied on fresh water pumped from the Delta. That water never reaches San Francisco Bay. Quenching people's thirst has transformed the chemistry of the whole estuary – and devastated its biota.

Water flow is not the only thing that changes the bay's chemistry. It's also subject to accidental additions: the by-products of industry and commerce. At Richmond, east of San Francisco, a refinery processes oil that comes and goes in tanker ships, and all of the enormous vessels that cross San Francisco Bay use oil as fuel. When ships collide (or hit other structures in the bay), oil seeps out of their punctured tanks. Chemistry furthers the catastrophe. Oil molecules are smaller than water molecules, so spilled oil floats and spreads over the bay. It coats shorebirds and mats the tiny hooks and barbs that make a watertight, airproof bond between their feathers.[2] Without that protective bond, a bird dies of exposure. The chemical structure of detergent has the power to save an oiled bird. Its molecules bond to both oil and water, so it washes the oil off the bird's feathers. Chemical accidents and chemical antidotes have immediate impacts on living systems.

Chemicals added to the bay on purpose are equally harmful, even when the process is less obvious and the consequences are delayed. As the US Navy's shipyards and nuclear laboratories discarded chemical waste offshore from Hunters Point, a witch's brew settled in layers of bay mud; it included petroleum fuels, pesticides, heavy metals, polychlorinated biphenals, volatile organic compounds, and radioactive material.[3] In 1989, the federal government declared the area a Superfund site, and a legal framework defined a process for forensic chemical analysis. Cores of mud were pulled from the bay floor and frozen for examination. Their contents allowed scientists (and the state) to trace pollutants, establish the sequence of pollution, assign responsibility, and prescribe measures for remediation. Without chemical detective work, chemical malfeasance would persist for the long term.

Analyzing and ameliorating the pollution at Hunters Point – and holding polluters accountable for what they had done – was possible because the contamination had bound-

---

2 "How Oil Affects Birds," from the website of International Bird Rescue.
3 "Treasure Island Naval Station—Hunters Point Annex San Francisco, CA: Cleanup Progress," from the website of the US EPA.

aries in space and time. Pollution over great distances and long intervals is too diffuse to manage, especially when chemistry intersects with processes of physics and biology. The mercury that pervades the bay began as the chemical mercury sulfide, locked in cinnabar rock near San Jose. Heated, the mercury sulfide gained energy and turned to vapor. Its chemical bonds were broken: sulphur detached from mercury and combined with oxygen to make sulphur dioxide, and elemental mercury was set free. When the vapor cooled and the elemental mercury lost energy, it became a liquid. Then, mining interests took mercury from San Jose to the Sierra Nevada to dissolve the gold trapped in ore. The process was chemical and physical. Mercury bonded with gold to make an amalgam. Energy – heat – added to the amalgam returned the mercury to a gaseous state. Cooled, the mercury became liquid again, and the process was repeated. Over decades of hydraulic mining, huge volumes of mercury flowed from the mountains to San Francisco Bay. Carried by water, mercury atoms lost electrons, and this change set the stage for their chemical transformation by living organisms. When they were metabolized by bacteria, the atoms bonded with carbon and hydrogen to form methyl mercury. That chemical transformation made the mercury easier to absorb, and it moved into the bay's fauna.

Mercury is a catalyst: it instigates chemical reactions without being consumed in the process. It has moved through San Francisco Bay's landscapes with and without people. It acted on and was acted upon by living and non-living systems; as that happened, it went through metamorphoses of form and meaning. People transformed it in ways best described by physics; they made use of it in ways best described by chemistry; and they unleashed consequences in ways best described by biology. Mercury is a reminder that the natural sciences examine the same world through different lenses. Each discipline tells its own version of the story.

Biology

Biology is the study of living organisms, or biota. Since Linnaeus, biologists have classified plants and animals according to a taxonomy of structural characteristics, but the edge of San Francisco Bay suggests a way of categorizing living creatures in direct connection to the landscape. That taxonomy, based on habitat and association, examines the relationships of biota to the physics and chemistry of the inanimate environment and to communities of other plants and animals, including people. It acknowledges that people shape – and share – the habitats of San Francisco Bay.

When the Aquatic Park bathhouse served as a swimmers' threshold between land and water, people changing clothes found themselves surrounded by images of other inhabitants of the bay. Some of them are almost human, kelp-wrapped mermen and mermaids who preside over anchors and ropes from forgotten shipwrecks. They float among a collection of dreamlike creatures: fish, squid, shells, snakes, turtles, corals, and plants that grow on the sea floor and float through the water. But the habitat of the imagination frees these beings from the specific relationships that flourish at the edge of the bay. There, plants and animals are tightly adapted to variations in salinity, elevation, soils, structures, food sources, and predators.

At more or less the same time that artists were conjuring the scenes at Aquatic Park, marine biologist Ed Ricketts devoted his book *Between Pacific Tides*[4] to the close observation and documentation of real life in the biotic neighborhoods of the bay. Ricketts identified a gradient of conditions that stretched between open water and dry land. He described ways in which non-living forces like wind, surf, exposure, and geological formation offered distinct habitats. He cataloged the plants and animals that lived together in each kind of habitat. He portrayed living things in relation to one another and to their contexts. Boundaries between the human and the non-human didn't trouble Ricketts; the conditions offered by an environment mattered more to him than their origins did. In his taxonomy, abandoned piers and pilings were habitats as important as rocks and tide pools.

Eighty years later, wildlife flourishes on human structures all along the edge of the bay. Below the working harbor (and beneath the level of most people's consciousness), the undersides of piers still offer homes to crabs, worms, nudibranchs, mussels, sea squirts, barnacles, algae, and tunicates.[5] Uphill, plants that grow in rocky soil flourish in the cracks in retaining walls. On the abandoned jetty at Heron's Head, riprap provided an armature for primary ecological succession. Sediment and sand piled up; birds dropped seeds; plants grew from the rubble; branches, leaves, fruits, and seeds provided shelter and food for avian, aquatic, terrestrial, and amphibious creatures. Animals have come to live all over Heron's Head, from under the water to the dry top of the jetty. People have a place there, too. Decades ago, they built the framework. These days, some tend to the marsh, others run a nature study center, and many come just to watch the birds and the tides.

---

4   Ricketts and Calvin, *Between Pacific Tides*.
5   Eric Simons, "The San Francisco Bay Is Wild Still," *Bay Nature*; "Chapter Eight: Submerged Aquatic Vegetation," *San Francisco Bay Subtidal Habitat Goals Report*.

No man is an island, and no plant or animal either. Every individual specimen is part of a web of connections. Even a single tree depends on complicated relationships with living and non-living systems. Minerals and microbes feed its roots. Water lets it convert the sun's physical energy into the chemical energy of sugars: photosynthesis. Air absorbs the oxygen and water that emerge from that process. Its leaves and branches make a place for birds and insects. A tree in San Francisco was likely planted by a person; as it grows, its shadow offers respite from the heat of a sunny day. When rain falls, the tree catches it and slows its progress into the ground – or into a pipe.

As they reach across the estuary of San Francisco Bay and its inland delta, the webs that connect living things to one another and to their environment become more and more complicated. Some creatures live their entire lives in and around the bay. Others pass through the estuary in processes linked to their life cycles; they move with the days, seasons and years. Shorebirds stop to rest or winter in the estuary on their way up and down the Pacific coast. Salmon and other anadromous fish live in the ocean as adults, but they spawn in rivers; reproduction takes them upstream and downstream through the bay.

Some migration follows human patterns. People introduced striped bass to the estuary in the late nineteenth century for fisheries; their proliferation has contributed to the decline of native species. Other invasives came as stowaways. Until the end of the twentieth century, the ballast water of ships brought flora and fauna from distant parts of the world into the bay. Without local predators, those species have made their way up the estuary and flourished at the expense of plants and animals native to the region; measures to kill the exotics would harm natives as well. Ten years ago, the Nature Conservancy found a higher proportion of invasive species in San Francisco Bay than in any other water body it had studied.[6] The biological processes launched by people – on purpose or by accident – have gone wild.

People's physical and chemical changes to the landscape escape control, too, and when that happens, living creatures bear the consequences. The impact can extend across habitats, communities, and generations – and watersheds. Mercury used as a mining catalyst in the Sierra Nevada mountains more than a century ago still affects the biota of San Francisco Bay. Its intersection with biological processes has transformed it into a poison, the neurotoxin methyl mercury. Absorbed by living tissues, methyl mercury works its way

---

6 Molnar et al., "Assessing the Global Threat."

through the food web: plankton eat the bacteria, small fish eat the plankton, big fish eat the small fish, and people and other large animals eat the big fish. As predators consume prey, they concentrate the contaminants: biomagnification. The bigger the predators and the longer they live, the higher the level of methyl mercury in their bodies and the greater the damage to their brains and kidneys.[7] Living creatures (including people) can't be separated from their environments or from the contexts of chemistry and physics. We are what we eat.

The value of fish as food makes wildlife a commodity. Settlers undertook commercial fishing on San Francisco Bay in the mid-nineteenth century. The industry was concentrated in 1900, when the State of California designated a stretch of San Francisco's northern shoreline as a landing place for commercial fishing boats. The edge of the bay between Taylor and Leavenworth Streets filled up with fishermen's stalls, factories for processing fish, and a market. In the nineteenth and early twentieth centuries, the varied catch included Chinook salmon, shad, sturgeon, clams, oysters, mussels, Pacific herring, northern anchovy, surfperch, shark, bay shrimp, and Dungeness crab. The catch has been reduced to fewer species, but it is still worth tens of millions of dollars every year.[8]

The California Department of Fish and Wildlife – until 2012 the Department of Fish and Game – hires scientists and interpreters with college educations in a telling series of fields in the natural and environmental sciences – zoology and botany, plus wildlife management and fisheries management. The agency's mission includes contradictory goals: "to manage California's diverse fish, wildlife, and plant resources, and the habitats upon which they depend, for their ecological values and for their use and enjoyment by the public."[9] Knowledge isn't neutral. Even when people pursue the natural sciences from pure curiosity, their knowledge is often turned toward practical purposes. Colonization and capitalism have turned the biota of the bay into an economic resource; public and private entities draw on science to make the more-than-human world useful and to inform assessments of what natural systems might be worth. We are what we eat – and what we catch and sell.

---

7   Canada's Ministry of the Environment and Climate Change offers detailed explanations of mercury's behavior in living and non-living systems in three website articles: "Mercury: Biogeochemistry," "Mercury in the Food Chain," and "Mercury: Health Concerns."
8   California Department of Fish and Wildlife, "2017-2018 California Commercial Herring Fishery FAQ Sheet" and "Table 10 – Monthly Landings in Pounds in the San Francisco Area During 2017"; Smith and Kato, "The Fisheries of San Francisco Bay."
9   Mission stated in the website of the California Department of Fish and Wildlife.

Keywords 3

Landscape as Resource

Since European and American settlers arrived in San Francisco Bay, they've defined the landscape as a resource, something of economic value. That interpretation underlay colonial claims to territory. It instigated the extraction of precious metals from the ground. It engendered trade in raw materials and, eventually, in many other things. The bay and the landscapes around it were worth defending because they could generate wealth.

Defense and commerce seem like terms of culture: they're human practices. The edge of the bay reveals them to be endeavors in which culture is deeply bound up with more-than-human systems. Making use of the landscape and protecting it from other people's claims have meant intervening in (and interfering with) its dynamic processes and patterns. Defense and commerce have remade the edge of the bay, and the unexpected consequences of that remaking have affected what people decide to defend and exchange, and how. Purposeful commerce in profitable goods has become inadvertent commerce in living creatures; defending the nation has given way to defending nature.

Defense

In the dictionary, defense means keeping something safe from danger or harm. It implies struggle (or the capacity for struggle) against forces that might capture or take away territory. Defense rests on the articulation of values: why is the territory worth safekeeping? It assumes the naming of enemies: who (or what) might take the territory away? The edge of the bay shows how changing values for the landscape redefine combatants.

San Francisco Bay offers examples of military defense, but the histories and aftermaths of military sites and the changing values of civilian culture have altered the collective understanding of threat and consequently, of protection. Defense has evolved along with public consciousness, but its latter-day expressions don't correspond to standard definitions. They operate undescribed, below the surface of collective perception.

Soldiers arrived in San Francisco Bay on the leading edge of colonization. The Spanish took control of the southern headlands of the Golden Gate – Fort Point – to guard access to the interior riches of California; the Mexicans followed them, and the Americans followed their example. Fort Point's location and elevation made it a vantage point to watch for enemies and if necessary, to shoot at them. It became the first in a constellation of forts with good views; the rest of the Presidio, Fort Mason, Angel Island, Alcatraz, Yerba Buena, Fort Baker, and Fort Barry defended the territorial boundaries of the United States against foreign and Confederate invaders. Fort Point fell into decline, but the others featured in a century's worth of conflict in the Pacific Theater: the Spanish-American War, the Second World War, the Korean War, and the Vietnam War.

All of that military land was restricted to military use. The army made significant changes at its bases – it put in fortifications, batteries, missile sites, parade grounds, housing, and roads – but large tracts of land remained undeveloped. Ecosystems paved over by urbanization in the rest of the Bay Area were preserved by neglect. In the 1950s and 1960s, as the army shifted its presence toward southern California, installations in San Francisco and its northern suburbs fell out of use. Developers made proposals, but the public saw the value of what had been preserved unintentionally and demanded protection for the bases' natural areas. In 1972 the federal government created the Golden Gate Recreation Area, the country's first urban national park, on an armature of former military land, including Fort Point. The vantage point for soldiers became a vantage point for citizens. The army had claimed the edge of the bay to defend it from foreign invasion; inadvertently, its occupation protected the headlands from the city.

The army defended its territory not only from the city but also from civilians. When the construction of the Golden Gate Bridge demanded an anchorage on the Presidio's headlands, just beside Fort Point, the viaduct of Doyle Drive served as a fortification against unauthorized visits to military land. It carried cars from the bridge to the city grid without touching the ground, and the Presidio remained *terra incognita* inside city limits. In 1989, culture and nature conspired to change the rules: Congress decided to close the Army base at the Presidio, and the Loma Prieta earthquake damaged the viaduct beyond repair. Five years later, when the Presidio was transferred to the Golden Gate National Recreation Area, it needed to be defended from the highway rather than from civilians. Reconceived as the Presidio Parkway, Doyle Drive's route has been rebuilt in tunnels whose roofs make a continuous ground plane from the shore to the hills. The roadway has ceased to be a boundary.

Boundaries define claims to land, and claims require defense. Fort Mason was built to defend the American claim to San Francisco Bay and territory inland. Like Fort Point, it commandeered a hill, Black Point, so that soldiers could survey the bay and guard it against invasion. In the early twentieth century, after the United States had expanded its claims into the Pacific, Fort Mason became part of a system that protected land offshore. Distant claims engendered a local one. Turning the fort into a point of embarkation for Pacific theaters of war meant building new land along the water's edge. That endeavor required three new boundaries within the fort. A retaining wall cut into Black Point made space for level ground with access to the bay. A seawall protected filled land from the tides. Pavement on the surface of the filled land separated water that flowed over it from water that saturated it. Those boundaries (and the claim they defend) are subject to attack by the landscape's dynamics. The retaining wall has to manage two threats: its foundation pushes back against the mass of the hill it holds back, and weepholes disperse water pooling in the retained earth. Unless it's raised, the seawall will succumb to sea level rise. The instability of filled land gives rise to cracks, and the only defense against crumbling pavement is constant maintenance. Earthworks and landfill mean war with land and water.

Ships fight a different battle: they have to contend with land that lies below water. The defense against submerged land turned Yerba Buena Shoals into Treasure Island. The shoals were threats to hulls, keels, rudders, and propellers; in some places, treacherous rock lay just a few feet under the water. To combat navigational hazards, the federal government built new land on top of the shoals. The underwater enemy became habitable territory. It was intended for a civilian airport, but the onset of the Second World War brought navy planes instead of commercial airliners. Conjured to defend ships from the uneven bay floor, Treasure Island became a military airbase to defend the Pacific Theater.

Fighting the Second World War depended on military bases around the bay. The prosecution of war at sea relied on the drydocks at Hunters Point, near San Francisco's southern boundary; defending the navy's ships from wear and tear was essential to national defense. Roosevelt's Great White Fleet docked at Hunters Point for maintenance in 1908, and the navy bought the shipyard from its civilian owners just before the Second World War. For the next four years, Hunters Point Naval Shipyard kept the Pacific Fleet in fighting condition.

After active battles gave way to the Cold War, national defense rested on deterrence – the idea that fear of retaliation would prevent a nuclear attack. In 1946, Hunters Point became the home of the Naval Radiological Defense Laboratory. For twenty-five years, military scientists and engineers investigated the physical and biological effects of nuclear and thermal radiation and worked on measures to counter them. The lab dumped contaminated waste at the shipyard, on the floor of San Francisco Bay, and just outside the Golden Gate. Research in support of nuclear defense became an attack on the environment.

What happened at Hunters Point was only one skirmish in a widespread war on American ecosystems. Landscapes across the United States were contaminated by military activities and industrial corporations. The collateral damage with respect to public health came to widespread attention in the 1970s. In 1980, Congress enacted a legislative defense: the Comprehensive Environmental Response, Compensation, and Liability Act. Nicknamed the Superfund, the act made polluters liable for the costs of cleaning up toxic sites. Hunters Point Naval Shipyard was added to the government's list of priorities in 1989 because of its contamination by radioactive material and an array of other harmful substances.[1] More than half of the 866 acres that need remediation are under water.[2] The naval base closed in 1994. Cleanup on its property continues.

The contamination at Hunters Point happened out of most people's sight; military boundaries kept civilians away from the shipyard. The federal government's map of the Superfund site draws a border around the base, too; it starts on dry land and continues on the bay floor. But a line on a drawing doesn't contain damage to the environment. Dumping in open water means dispersal. At the Presidio, the rhetoric of Doyle Drive said that military and civilian life were separate. The mud offshore from Hunters Point speaks the truth: that division has always been a fiction. The armed forces are part and parcel of the culture at large – and of the culture's confrontation with land and water.

The front line in that contest is physical and ideological: a seawall defends the city's margin from Fort Point to Hunters Point. Building the seawall claimed territory from the marshes and tidal flats that had comprised the shore. Though it seemed (and still seems) to have turned a wild, ambiguous, irregular edge into something controlled and tame, the war's not over. The highest high tides already wash over marina steps, and sea level rise threatens all the land the seawall captured from the bay. That claim, almost six and a half of the city's forty-nine square miles of land,[3] includes San Francisco's commercial armature: wharves, factories, and the Financial District.

The word armature comes from the Latin word *armatura*, meaning military equipment or arms. Plans to rebuild the seawall are underway, and the project received federal

1 US EPA, "Treasure Island Naval Station."
2 Naval Facilities Engineering Command, "Former Naval Shipyard Hunters Point."
3 Measured from Figure 3 of Chin, Wong and Carlson, "Shifting Shoals and Shattered Rocks," 4.

funding in June 2018.[4] Current data suggest that global warming and glacier melting may outpace the construction of defenses against sea level rise.[5] Even so, the idea of retreat from land built by and for commerce remains unthinkable to people with a stake in shoreline real estate. The financial value of what they've gained is too high to surrender.

Commerce

In the dictionary, commerce means the individual exchange of one item of value for another and the collective aggregation of those exchanges. It requires the establishment of relative values among different kinds of objects and ideas, from raw materials and manufactured goods to computer code and money. In capitalist economies, values arise from what people are willing to pay: the market. Commercial transactions seem like acts of pure culture. In the early nineteenth century, as the Industrial Revolution and colonial trade fueled British consumption, William Wordsworth wrote,

> The world is too much with us; late and soon,
> Getting and spending, we lay waste our powers; –
> Little we see in Nature that is ours; [...][6]

Wordsworth's sonnet portrays manufactured things as distractions from the beauty of the wind, the sea, and the moon; it argues that the business of buying and selling alienates people from the more-than-human world. Seen another way, the processes of production and consumption (and the commerce those processes give rise to) are completely bound up with the environment. They rest on the translation of raw materials – natural resources – into objects of desire, goods for purchase and sale.

The story of today's shoreline begins with that kind of translation, when gold pulled from the Sierra Nevada mountains was traded for food, manufactured goods, and cash. San Franciscans remade the edge of the bay so that ships carrying goods could come and go, warehouses could provide a place to store those goods, and banks could make money

4 Taylor Griffin, "Pelosi Announces Federal Funding for San Francisco's Embarcadero Seawall," on the website of Congresswoman Nancy Pelosi.
5 San Francisco's complete defense against sea level rise won't be finished till 2046. The plan is laid out in Office of the City Administrator, Office of Resilience and Capital Planning, *Fortifying San Francisco's Great Seawall*.
6 William Wordsworth, *The World Is Too Much With Us*, ll. 1–3.

available. The city's first markets dealt in objects: raw materials and finished goods. Trade expanded to funds: stocks, bonds, and mortgages. Now it centers on ideas and experiences: software, or dinner in a restaurant on the pier. Changes in commerce change the landscape too, sometimes according to plan and sometimes by surprise.

San Francisco was born an entrepot. The bay connected the rest of the world to the riches of California's interior. For twenty years after the Gold Rush, until the transcontinental railroad was finished, the only route between California and the east coast of the United States was by sea. Ships began arriving as soon as gold was discovered. They landed at the Mexican pueblo at Yerba Buena Cove, where geography offered shelter from prevailing winds. Trade supported mining and urbanization. Equipment, food, and building materials came in; gold went out.[7]

The cove had enabled commerce, and commerce transformed the cove. Constant traffic demanded the port's expansion, but fast growth meant provisional construction. Buildings were set on pilings, mudflats were filled with sand and debris, and boats tied to piers or dragged onto the mud served as *ad hoc* warehouses, offices, and boarding houses. In 1851, fire destroyed most of the assemblage. Piers, buildings, and ships collapsed into mud and shallow water, and the rapid filling of new land preserved their ruins. Yerba Buena Cove still lies beneath the tall buildings of the Financial District; getting and spending continue high above the buried ships of San Francisco's first commercial neighborhood.[8]

The Financial District's streets are urban canyons, long, cool, dark, narrow spaces that evoke the experience of mountain gorges. Their connection to the mountains rests on more than metaphor: gold pulled out of the Sierra Nevada range gave birth to San Francisco's finance industry. Banking culture emerged because miners needed to value, store, and move their gold; they had to buy supplies and send their earnings home. To meet those needs, gold dealers, general merchants, and express agents bought safes, issued certificates of exchange, and built solid buildings that signaled trustworthiness: banks.[9] When the Gold Rush took off, San Francisco's port became the center of trade and transport between northern California and the rest of the world. Banks clustered there, and they stayed even after the transcontinental railroad arrived at Oakland two decades later. Wells Fargo, now one of the largest financial institutions in the world, started as an express company. It began issuing certificates of exchange in 1852 from offices across gold

---

7   Jackson, "The Early Historical Geography of San Francisco." See also Delgado, *Gold Rush Port.*
8   Delgado's *Gold Rush Port* describes the fire and its traces.
9   Schweikart and Pierson-Doti, "From Hard Money to Branch Banking."

country. A year later it opened an office in San Francisco.[10] That building still stands, just down the street from the bank's towering glass-and-steel headquarters. The rise of such monuments to commerce and finance is built on the fall of mountains. Extracting gold tore the Sierra Nevada apart.

Commerce of all kinds meets San Francisco Bay at the Embarcadero. When the road was laid along the city's seawall, it allowed truck and rail traffic between and beyond the wharves and warehouses that lined the shore. A seam between land and water, it supported maritime trade on a working waterfront; it connected ships and piers to brokerages, shops, and banks. A century later, business along the Embarcadero has taken new forms. Some changes came with shifts in the global landscape. As container shipping turned Oakland into the bay's main port, work on the wharves dwindled. Then, as heavy industry moved overseas, San Francisco's economy turned from manufacturing to finance, tourism, and information technology. Other changes followed a local seismic shift. After the Loma Prieta earthquake left the Embarcadero Freeway unsafe, the elevated highway was taken down. It had blocked the city's view of San Francisco Bay for more than three decades. In today's economy, where the Embarcadero supports commerce related to leisure and pleasure, that view has resource value. Restaurants and bars trade on the beauty of the landscape: people pay to see the water.

The restaurants at Fisherman's Wharf represent an intersection between commerce in raw materials and commerce in experience. The restaurants rely on local fishermen who pull fish and shellfish out of the water just as miners pulled precious metals from mountainsides. Like gold, the animals have become a commodity, a valuable natural resource consumed by the restaurants' patrons. The word consume has a range of meanings: to *eat* or *devour* or *swallow up*, but also to *destroy, exhaust, expend, waste, squander*, and *use up*. Commerce in gold consumed the mountains; commerce in the bay's aquatic creatures consumes their living communities. Regardless, diners enjoy what's on their plates – and more. They consume the view of the water, the spectacle of the pier, the romance of something just captured from the wild, and the luxury of someone else's cooking. Pleasure has turned into a product. Commercial transactions at Fisherman's Wharf take place at the scale of the body, person by person and fish by fish. They're intimate. What's extracted from the landscape becomes part of the person who consumes it.

---

10 See the article "Gold Rush Roots of Wells Fargo" on the website of Wells Fargo.

Commerce at the Port of Oakland takes place at another order of magnitude, the scale of the globe. The port is the region's center of trade with the world. In 2016, 77 percent of its business was with Asia, 12 percent with Europe, 7 percent with Hawaii and Guam, and 2 percent with Australia, New Zealand, and Oceania.[11] The vast industrial harbor doesn't look like the impromptu scene at Yerba Buena Cove, but some things haven't changed since the Gold Rush. The biggest exports, food products like fruits, nuts, grains, meat, and fish, still rely on natural resources: soil and water. Most of what arrives is still manufactured goods.[12] Automation, offshore production, and cheap shipping have multiplied the volumes of exchange and consumption far beyond Wordsworth's imagination, and all of this getting and spending has had an unexpected consequence. Until the turn of the twenty-first century, the purposeful exchange of items of value was accompanied by the inadvertent exchange of living creatures through ballast water. Commerce has turned San Francisco Bay and its estuary into the world's most invaded aquatic ecosystem.

Wordsworth was mistaken when he wrote, "Little we see in Nature that is ours." Starting with the Gold Rush, commerce along the edge of the bay has proceeded from the assumption that everything we see in nature *is* ours: to take, to sell, to use, to consume. And when people look at more-than-human systems in and around San Francisco Bay, much of what they – we – see belongs to us too. It's the unwitting product of our own doings.

11 "Facts & Figures" on the website of the Port of Oakland Seaport.
12 "What's in the Box? Top Commodities at the Port of Oakland," on the website of the Port of Oakland Seaport.

Keywords 4

Means of Domestication, Settlement, Urbanization

Geography made San Francisco Bay a center of commerce, and commerce brought enough people to make a city. The settlers who built San Francisco worked to domesticate the bay and its edges. To make the environment predictable and stable, they developed ways of describing and taming places they perceived as uncharted and wild, and in some ways they succeeded. But the human transformation of the bay is a work in progress. Interventions in a landscape's dynamic systems don't stop change; unexpected consequences at local and global scales push back on cultural expectations. Since the Gold Rush, people have shaped the edge of San Francisco Bay to meet their own priorities and ambitions. Sea level rise is reversing the paradigm: looking forward, living on the shoreline will require cultural values and practices to change with the evolving landscape.

Navigation

The dictionary says that navigation has to do with making, finding, or traveling over a planned route. Its origins are Latin: *navis* is "ship," and *agere* is "to drive," so *navigare* is "to sail" or "to make a voyage."

Navigation is an endeavor in parts. People find a route through a landscape they don't know, and then they represent information about what they've found. The representations allow other people to follow the same course (and, if they want, to add their own notes). A sailor navigating San Francisco Bay depends on past voyages and shared knowledge. The knowledge she acquires from her predecessors' journeys colors her experience, and so does the knowledge she gains first-hand. Navigation is a reiterative practice.

As we make our way in a landscape, the way changes. Navigated territory becomes a legible text. Charts and maps bring order to environments. They turn places where we're strangers into landscapes to be traveled through. Everyday metaphor recognizes this: uncharted means unknown – and risky. Even places that remain beyond control are different after they've been deciphered and described. The sea is always wild, but once navigated, it's no longer a wilderness.

Navigation needs visible, stable points that a navigator can find again. Located, named, and shared on maps and through stories, those features begin to pin down and tame unknown places. The colonial domestication of San Francisco Bay began in 1775, when a Spanish ship's captain sailed through the headlands at its entrance. A distinctive hill at the northeast corner of the San Francisco Peninsula marked the way to the sheltered harbor at Yerba Buena Cove, and he called it Loma Alta: High Hill. Named on early maps of the bay and shoreline, the place became part of the common knowledge of sailors who followed the captain: a landmark.

Since then, the landmark has shared other kinds of knowledge. The high hill offered views of the Golden Gate and the harbor, and the Marine Telegraph, a semaphore at its top, could be seen from both places. When ships entered the bay, the operator of the semaphore set its arms in code that telegraphed their type and condition to people in the harbor. The power of that signal gave the landmark a new name: Telegraph Hill. After the electromagnetic telegraph came into use, the semaphore pole supported a time ball that told ship captains how to calibrate their navigation instruments.[1] The apparatus no longer announced who was arriving in San Francisco Bay, but it gave ships information essential to their departure.

Twentieth-century constructions have changed Telegraph Hill and its signals. In 1908, a giant welcome sign conveyed San Francisco's sentiments to the Great White Fleet. Twenty-five years later, Coit Tower turned the landmark into a destination. The building has made Telegraph Hill even easier to spot, and its observatory frames views in every direction. On the way up, visitors pass paintings of what they'll see: the hills of the Bay Area, the waterfront, Alcatraz, Marin County, Yerba Buena Island, and ferries plying the bay. From far away, the tower helps a person find her place in the landscape; from inside, it tells her how to look at it.

Landmarks like Telegraph Hill depend on sight. When fog covers San Francisco Bay, it renders them invisible. The landscape would be returned to illegible wilderness if sailors couldn't find their way by hearing. The foghorns on the Golden Gate Bridge serve as aural landmarks. Horns on each of the bridge's two towers send out signals at different intervals and tones: their sounds represent their locations. Pilots and sailors who understand the code know how to avoid the towers. They steer between the sounds on their way to port and north of the sounds on their way to sea.

Navigation by foghorn is an exchange between actors and instruments. An operator turns on the horns, and vibrating membranes inside send sound waves through the fog.

---

1 Myrick, *San Francisco's Telegraph Hill*, 28, 32.

The sound waves travel to the membranes in the ears of pilots, and the pilots interpret what they hear. Their interpretations keep their ships on course; unseen and unseeing, the ships sail past one another and the bridge.

Soundings are not sounds, but they too provide a way of showing what can't be seen. Sound comes from a Latin word, *sonus,* which means *noise, voice,* or *tone.* Sounding comes from two Latin words, *sub,* which means under, and *unda,* which means wave: soundings measure the distance between the surface of a water body and its floor. The US Office of Coast Survey has been sounding San Francisco Bay point by point since 1850. The first measurements were made with poles and lead lines extended from a boat until they touched the bottom of the bay. Today, SONAR[2] brings together sounds and soundings. Its instruments put out sound waves at a known frequency. As the waves hit the bay floor and bounce back to the instruments, formulas calculate distance from the duration of the round trip.

Sounds (and sights) are unmediated information: navigators rely on their own hearing (or vision) to find their way. Soundings require translation onto nautical charts to be legible. Charts map water bodies and their edges. Sounding depths are plotted where they were measured, and contour lines connect points at the same depth. The pattern of contour lines represents underwater topography. Charts and contours represent the bay floor as an abstraction, not an image. Soundings aren't landmarks.

Charts of San Francisco Bay are evidence that navigators care more about what happens on and under water than on land: they read as opposites to maps of the terrestrial landscape. Streets only appear where they connect to the shoreline, and the ground looks flat and empty. But the area off shore is full of information. Numbers and lines stand for a world that can't be seen or heard; they make the bay floor legible. A chart brings together knowledge. Because charts are produced by government agencies, that knowledge becomes a standard. As it circulates, the chart standardizes understanding – and perception.

Landmarks let navigators read the landscape by sight, foghorns let them read the landscape by sound, and soundings let them read the landscape by chart. In a sailboat, a navigator needs another kind of literacy: he has to read the wind. In fact, he reads a translation. Wind is invisible, but a careful watcher can register its effects. Ripples in the water show its direction, and a tell-tale on a boat's mast reveals whether a sail has caught the wind correctly. Winds change from moment to moment, so sailing means constant observation and response. It's a negotiation among sailor, wind, and water, mediated by

---

2 The acronym for "sound navigation and ranging."

a boat with sails, spar, and keel. Or perhaps it's an appropriation: sails (and sailors) capture wind.

Now only pleasure boats navigate under sail. Petroleum moves the big ships on San Francisco Bay, and tugboats keep them on course. Digital charts and GPS provide increasingly sophisticated information, but reaching shore still means navigating hazards. Offshore, winds blow toward the rocky coast; a sandbar complicates the Golden Gate; fog obscures the view; currents are fast and unpredictable; the floor of the bay shifts; clearances are tight; and traffic is heavy no matter the weather. Safe passage demands the deep knowledge that comes from local experience. To enter or leave the bay, ships have to take on pilots licensed by the state. The pilots are experts, but the crossing still requires their full attention, careful observation, nuanced interpretation, and informed action. The bay is no longer a wilderness, but it remains wild.

The worst hazard on the bay is bad judgment: the wildness within us. Human error under difficult circumstances has produced wrecks twice in the last fifty years. Once, two ships collided; once, a ship hit the tower of the Bay Bridge. Both times, oil poured out of pierced fuel tanks, covered the water, and coated and killed thousands of shorebirds.[3] Navigation is a negotiation with the inanimate environment – water, wind, weather, rocks, shoals, bridge towers – and when the negotiation fails, what lives in the environment becomes collateral damage.

Sooner or later, all navigators need to return to land. Before the Gold Rush, the bay's shallow, fluctuating mudflats and tidal marshes made it hard for boats with fixed keels or deep drafts to reach the shore. Ports were designed for the smooth arrival and departure of maritime traffic. Piers extended into deep water; new land filled the flats and marshes; lighthouses signaled the shoreline; breakwaters dampened the force of waves; wharves provided mooring places; gangplanks carried people from boats to landings; and drydocks repaired ships. The harbor became a haven between voyages.

Freighters and pleasure craft still sail into the bay, but airplanes have mostly replaced passenger ships. Like boats, planes allow people to leave solid ground, and they too need places to embark and land. Commercial flights began in the 1930s with Pan Am's flying

---

3 The accidents received coverage in the local and national press when they occurred. Long-term consequences to birds have been reported by International Bird Rescue, the Oiled Wildlife Care Network, and Wildcare Bay Area. Fish incurred damage as well; see the following articles for details: International Bird Rescue, "Cosco Busan Bird Toll Update; Plovers Survive Spill," *International Bird Rescue*, 26 January 2010; Mike Ziccardi, "Cosco-Busan Oil Spill," *Oiled Wildlife Care Network*, 7 November 2012; Cosco Busan Oil Spill Trustees, Cosco Busan *Oil Spill Final Damage Assessment and Restoration Plan/Environmental Assessment*; Elizabeth Devitt, "Explaining the Cosco Busan Spill's Toxic Effects: Scientists Report a Link between Oil and Fish Heart Health," *Bay Nature*, 9 April 2014; Incardona et al. "Unexpectedly High Mortality."

boats, seaplanes that came and went from the cove between Treasure Island and Yerba Buena Island. Named China Clippers after fast nineteenth-century sailing ships, they carried mail and passengers across the Pacific weekly. The metaphor of water has outlasted the seaplanes. Modern aircraft use runways, but they still land at a port: an airport.

Navigating by boat has given way to cars as well as planes. Before the Bay Bridge, people traveled between San Francisco and Oakland by ferry; crossing San Francisco Bay meant engaging the water. Connected to highways on both sides of the bay, the bridge turned the Bay Area into an automobile landscape. Highways have grown into freeways, and crossing the bay means navigating a maze of interchanges.[4] Drivers count on landmarks to confirm they're on the right track. Heading east, the cranes at the Port of Oakland announce the shoreline ahead; heading west, Telegraph Hill still signals the approach to San Francisco. Navigation means finding a way through the constructed landscape as well as the wilderness.

Construction

Ports, airports, bridges, and highways all belong to a landscape constructed around San Francisco Bay. Construction's origins are Latin: *con-* means together, and *struere* is to lay or pile up. To construct something is to assemble it from parts. The edge of the bay is an assembly created to allow intense inhabitation. Buildings are not the only built things in that *mise en scène*. People have manufactured and manipulated the ground; traffic and water flow through engineered conduits; and ideas about the landscape's meaning take shape and evolve with collective values and desires.

The tall buildings in San Francisco's Financial District are constructions that make money. The greater the number of stories, the more rent a building can generate (at least, in principle). The more distinctive the shape, the greater the building's power as a landmark on the skyline – and as a symbol of prominent corporate tenants. Everything about tall buildings is manufactured: the steel and concrete in their frames, the glass in their skins, the regular geometry of their forms, the standardized spaces that show through their illuminated windows at night. Hidden structures support what's visible: high-rises at the edge of the bay need deep foundations because the land they're built on is also a fabrication. The places where tall buildings stand now were tidelands until Americans

---

4 91 million trips were made across the Bay Bridge in the 2014–15 fiscal year. See "San Francisco-Oakland Bay Bridge" on the website of the Metropolitan Transportation Commission.

colonized San Francisco Bay. Settlers made new ground to build the city, but the assemblage underfoot doesn't have the strength to hold up high-rises. The Financial District is a construction on a construction.

The ground uphill from the shore is a found object rather than a fabrication, but its surface has been remade in the service of the city. The bedrock hills of the Coast Range were too steep to build on until cut, fill, and retention walls turned their slopes into terraces. The new topography offers level building sites and redistributes elevations so that streets run at consistent angles. On hills too steep for cars, streets turn into stairways. The stairs and streets give form to a conversation between two kinds of geometry: the simple logic of a grid and the complex curves of the native terrain. The pitch of streets changes from block to block, often significantly, but all intersections are level. Punctuated by horizontal squares, the warped net of lines makes an abstract representation of the hills.

The construction of buildings and streets for people requires the construction of spaces for water. Before San Francisco was built, rain flowed to the bay over land and through marshes; sometimes it traveled through streams, and sometimes it soaked into the ground and seeped out. Now the surface of the city controls water more tightly. Roofs and roads shed rain into gutters and drains, and pipes and sewers underground carry it to the bay. Marina Green offers clues to that hidden system: metal plates that say WATER. They look like plaques in the park's lawn, but they cover openings to an enormous vault that stores drainage from the north part of San Francisco. The perfect plane of grass is the roof of a building made for rain.

Beneath Marina Green, water from the city is contained on its way to the bay. Beneath the Palace of Fine Arts, water from the bay seeps freely through the constructed ground of the city. Imperceptible on the surface, the water underground rises and falls with the tides. It blurs the boundary of the bay's constructed edge.

The Palace of Fine Arts blurs boundaries, too. It muddies distinctions between places, between buildings and land, between past and present, and between the material world and the world of ideas. The palace occupies a surface that came from somewhere else. Its grounds are a third-generation construction descended from new land built at San Francisco's harbor and from buildings erected on that unsteady terrain.

When the earthquake of 1906 shook the new land, the buildings collapsed; fire finished them off. Rebuilding meant hauling wreckage from the harbor's edge to the marshes on San Francisco's northern shore. That rubble built new land; the filled marshes became fairgrounds for a World's Fair conceived to announce San Francisco's recovery. Displaced and reassembled, the ruins of the everyday city made a place for the urban fantasy of the fair.

The palace has simultaneous lives as a physical construction and as an assemblage of ideas and images. Designed to resemble a classical temple in decay, the building represents things that withstand time; its ancestors and inspirations stood (and still stand) in Greece and Rome. It's a replica, too, the concrete reproduction of a plaster of Paris original made for the World's Fair. That structure was fragile, but it conjured substance; it was new, but it evoked the distant past. Plaster or concrete, the palace lives in constant relation to an image of the moment: the shimmering reflection it casts in the lagoon next door.

The Palace of Fine Arts illuminates construction's parallel processes. Above ground and below, the act of building mediates between the landscape as people find it and as they imagine it might be. The constructions at the edge of the bay refer to ideas about the past – and the future.

Infrastructure

Ideas underlie more than individual constructions; they also account for infrastructure, the networks that support contemporary life. Translated directly from its Latin components, infrastructure means "below structure;" the word appeared in French in 1875 to describe the subgrade of a railway line. Imported into English, it has come to designate a range of things: roads, bridges, telephone lines, the power grid, the water supply, the sewer system. But the edge of the bay shows that infrastructure is not only a collection of objects. The landscape's physical systems rest on constellations of concepts and practices. San Francisco's seawalls emerged from notions about property; its aqueduct was built because of a belief in the right to water; and the efficacy of its foghorns depends on the work of operators and pilots. Whatever form it takes, infrastructure is never fully fixed. It embodies the endless negotiation between people's plans for the landscape and environmental forces they can't contain.

The edge of San Francisco Bay is an artefact produced by negotiation with the tides. Before the middle of the nineteenth century, the margins of the bay flooded twice a day. Tidelands were too wet to buy and sell until the conceptual infrastructure of the law supported their conversion to private property. In 1850 the US Congress granted title to overflowed lands to American states; a year later, the California legislature allowed the transfer of ownership to citizens who agreed to raise the ground above high tide.

A network of ideas had made the tidelands into places that could be exchanged for money, but the establishment of real estate along the shore required the physical infrastructure of the seawall. Built between 1860 and 1910, the seawall followed the mean low tide line. Taller than high tide, it provided a stable boundary for rock and rubble piled on tidal flats to make new land. That ground supported commerce and industry, and it provided the route for a freeway that connected San Francisco to suburbs across the bay and down the peninsula. The infrastructure of ideas about property operated uphill from the shore, too. It underlay the retaining walls that turned San Francisco's steep slopes into valuable building sites.

Walls that turn land into parcels look more certain than they are. Dynamic environmental processes make infrastructure impermanent. The seawall can't prevent the bay from saturating filled land. It didn't provide enough structure to prevent earthquake damage in 1906 and 1989, when the new ground lost strength and stiffness and buildings and a highway were damaged beyond repair. Uphill, retaining walls don't stop movement in the ground. Soil settles slowly with gravity and suddenly with earthquakes. Water flows through pores in the soil. Tree roots claim space as they grow. Shifting earth cracks the walls; colonized by plants that like dry, rocky soil, the cracks grow and spread. Untended, the retaining walls would lose their hold on the hills. Retention requires maintenance: a wall's durability depends on the work of the person who patches it. Infrastructure consists of practices as well as objects – and practices, unlike objects, can respond to changing circumstances.

Sometimes the relationship between objects and practices turns infrastructure into a performance. The theater is in the sky and on the water. The stage is set when dense, low fog covers the bay and obscures the towers of the Golden Gate Bridge.[5] There are two roles: the foghorn operator and the bar pilot. Watching from the bridge deck, the operator starts the horns when fog rolls in. They sound over the bay (and across the city), and their code tells the pilot which way to go. When the fog lifts, the operator turns the horns off. The sky falls quiet, and the pilot navigates by sight – and by way of the infrastructure of information: nautical charts, tide tables, and an understanding of physics that lets him steer a ship with the weights and counterweights of tugboats. A pilot's practices depend on representations and ideas as well as objects.

Most of the pilots on San Francisco Bay travel to and from the Port of Oakland, where the relationship between objects and practices has had unexpected consequences. The port's systems were designed to provide predictable conditions for the exchange of goods. Trucks and trains meet ships more than a thousand feet long; giant cranes move containers landward and seaward. But the port's infrastructure has created uncontrollable relationships among the bay's biota. Empty and partly loaded ships carry ballast water that

---

5 Sam Whiting, "When the Foghorns Blow," *SF Gate*, July 10, 2009.

brings plant and animal stowaways from a voyage's point of origin. Until the turn of the twenty-first century, when legal infrastructure changed port protocols,[6] exotic flora and fauna came straight to Oakland, established themselves in San Francisco Bay, migrated up the estuary, and wrought havoc on local ecosystems. New regulations limit further invasion, but they can't solve the existing problem. Infrastructural practices changed too slowly for the living systems of the bay and estuary.

At the Port of Oakland, careless practices wrought havoc with habitat, but across the bay at Heron's Head, carelessness allowed habitat to emerge and flourish. In 1970, the Port of San Francisco began to build the landing jetty for a southern bay bridge: physical infrastructure. Seven years later, the proposal for the new crossing was defeated in a referendum: legislative infrastructure. The abandonment of an idea meant the abandonment of what had been constructed. For almost two decades no one cared for the jetty, and a marsh began to thrive. Then the law came into play. A settlement to redress environmental damage required the port authority to cultivate the unexpected wilderness; people paid by port funds still tend its flora and fauna.[7] Infrastructure exists in relation to culture. Like the jetty, objects change their meaning as values change; like the marsh, accidents become gardens once people care about them.

Shifts in values complicate infrastructure. The laws and ideas that underlay the construction of San Francisco's aqueduct have come into conflict with newer laws and ideas that support the protection of the environment. The aqueduct mediates between people and what might be the largest and most ephemeral of environmental processes, the climate. Central California's summers are dry, and even rainy winters don't provide enough water to sustain large populations. In the 1920s and 1930s, San Francisco's public utility commission built a system to capture drinking water from the Sierra Nevada mountains, where snow and rain are abundant. The Hetch-Hetchy Dam impounds water, and an engineered system of conduits, reservoirs, and pumps delivers it to town. It diverts water that would otherwise flow through rivers down the mountains, through California's Great Central Valley, and into the delta that feeds San Francisco Bay.

The water system is fixed, but the living systems of the landscape aren't. Water for the metropolis arrives at the expense of the largest estuary on the west coast of the Americas, and aquatic species essential to its ecosystem are in the late stages of collapse. The public

---

6 Since 2000, the Ballast Water Management for Control of Nonindigenous Species Act (California Assembly Bill 703) has prohibited ships from releasing non-indigenous species into US territorial waters. To that end, the California State Lands Commission has established protocols for the management of ballast water. See US Department of the Interior, *California Coastal National Monument*, 3.20-4.

7 Bay Conservation and Development Commission, *Agreement*. For a summary of the events leading up to the agreement, see Pete Holloran's article, "India Basin and the Southeast Bayshore," on the website of *FoundSF*.

has finally registered the loss, and the original negotiation between people and climate has become a negotiation among people with plural values about who has first rights to the water, citizens or fish.[8] Metropolitan growth and climate change will raise the stakes. The aqueduct has become a question: how should people share the landscape and its resources with one another and with other creatures?

Defining infrastructure means reckoning with time. Some intervals are measured in human terms. The port and the aqueduct changed living systems in a few generations, and the jetty at Heron's Head changed meaning in a few decades. The Bay Bridge speaks to time at geological scales: it connects with bedrock. Three or four million years ago, tectonic movement formed the hills that surround and punctuate San Francisco Bay. Ten thousand years ago, the last Ice Age ended and the valley between two chains of hills became a bay. One hundred and seventy years ago, give or take, San Francisco and Oakland were established on either side. Eighty-four years ago, the Bay Bridge created a strip of continuous ground across the watery center of the metropolis. The bridge defied landmass, but its suspension spans were anchored in the solid rock of Rincon Hill and Yerba Buena Island. Its deck was hung from cables pulled tight at both points (and at a third, constructed anchorage); cables and towers transfer the weight of the structure to bedrock far below the shifting bay floor.

The cars driving back and forth between San Francisco and Oakland are twentieth-century inventions, but most of them run on a substance whose origins are hundreds of millions of years old. Gasoline, a fossil fuel, derives from ancient marine creatures. Buried under sediment and rock, the carbon in their bodies turned to oil. Refined and burned in internal combustion engines, it contributes to the warming of Earth's atmosphere. Since 1936, countless trips across the bay have added to the making of a geological era shaped by human action: the Anthropocene. Treasure Island, constructed just below the Bay Bridge, owes the rock in its seawall to the tunnel that connects the western and eastern spans across Yerba Buena Island. Treasure Island emerged from the bay in 1937, the year after the bridge opened. The National Oceanic and Atmospheric Agency's intermediate-level sea level rise scenario puts a quarter of the island underwater by the end of this century. In its extreme scenario, the island will be all but gone in fifty years.[9]

Culture has changed the landscape of San Francisco Bay: it built islands and sent cars across bridges. But infrastructure remains a negotiation in process, and the landscape of the Anthropocene will change the objects, practices, and ideas that have allowed people to live at the water's edge.

---

8 Lauren Sommer, "San Francisco Is Fighting California's Plan to Save Salmon. Wait. What?," *NPR*, 22 May 2011.
9 "Sea Level Rise Viewer," *NOAA*.

Keywords 5

Life from Day to Day

What does it mean to live at the edge of the bay? How does the landscape color a person's experience from day to day, and how does collective experience shape the landscape in return? Freud said, "Love and work are the cornerstones of our humanness."[1] Translated to San Francisco's shoreline, work includes things done for utility (or money). In the nineteenth century, that meant extracting, trading, and processing natural resources. Today, in the fields of finance and computing, it involves squeezing wealth from numbers. Whatever the endeavor, the work that dominates the scene requires support: there are always workers behind workers. Things done for love translate as play. They're expressions of delight undertaken without practical ends.

Boundaries at the edge of the bay seem blurrier than in Freud's formulation. Work and play mix and vary. Sometimes work becomes play, and sometimes play depends on work. People's understandings of utility and pleasure emerge from their own readings of the shoreline. Those readings change the landscape; as the landscape changes, daily life changes, too.

Work

To work is to do something. Germanic in origin, the word refers to action, labor, and employment.[2] In physics, work measures the transfer of energy; it takes place when a force moves an object along a path.[3] In everyday life, its dictionary definitions involve effort expended to achieve a result, especially with respect to earning a living.

---

1 In his essay "Apocryphal Freud: Sigmund Freud's Most Famous 'Quotations' and Their Actual Sources," Alan Elms reports that this elegant formulation did not appear in print until after Freud's death and was likely the work of Erik Erikson. Originally published in *The Annual of Psychoanalysis* 29 (2001): 83–104, the essay is available on Dr Elms's Web page at the University of California, Davis.

2 *Oxford English Dictionary*, s.v. "Work."

3 For an elegant analysis of work and energy in a hybrid landscape, see White, *The Organic Machine*.

When European and American settlers arrived at the edge of the bay, their work centered on the extraction, exploitation, refinement, and trade of natural resources. Now the environment provides a scenic backdrop for white-collar enterprises and tourism. The waterfront sums up the story of the national economy: service, technology, and consumption have replaced industry and manufacturing, and the landscape has changed with the culture. On most of San Francisco's wharves, waiters and cleaners have replaced longshoremen and factory workers. In the leisure economy, some work so that others can play.

From San Francisco's establishment until the 1970s, work on the waterfront was related to the coming and going of boats. Each pier and wharf acted as a fulcrum between land and sea. Ships docked and embarked; they were loaded and unloaded; and their contents were put into or taken from warehouses. The Embarcadero allowed the transport of goods along shore, and it connected ships and docks to banks, brokers, and merchants. Traffic at the harbor generated industry. Some enterprises, like shipyards, ropeyards, and barrel-makers, supported maritime activity. Others served broader markets; factories along the shore produced iron, steel, mining equipment, sugar, and electrical power.

Work on the waterfront meant physical exertion. Seamen, riggers, and pilots sailed ships to and from port. Stevedores lifted cargo off boats, longshoremen moved it along the piers, and warehouse workers handled goods on land. Drydockers built and repaired ships. Craftsmen and factory hands made raw materials into finished goods. Labor on San Francisco's wharves produced ideas as well as objects. Longshoreman philosopher Eric Hoffer wrote about social psychology in ways that influenced national culture. Harry Bridges founded the International Longshoremen's and Warehousemen's Union, which organized waterfront laborers up and down the Pacific coast. Ethical and militant, he shaped the American union movement and made important gains for workers across the country.

The landscape of work and the landscape of the shoreline changed together. In the 1980s, as the economy of the United States shifted from industry to service, jobs moved from docks to high-rises. Banks and businesses employed people in office buildings on the Embarcadero's landward side. People worked just a short walk from the water's edge without any connection to the bay. In the 1990s, after the Embarcadero Freeway came down, the threshold between land and water came to life in a new way. After thirty years of separation by cars and concrete, San Francisco's center was reconnected to its fringe of piers and wharves. Container shipping had moved the bay's main port to Oakland, and factories had left for cheaper locales offshore. The waterfront became a site of consumption rather than production. On the Embarcadero, the freight railroad has given way to a historic-looking streetcar; restaurants, bars, and tourist attractions occupy the wharves and warehouses. Harry Bridges still casts a metaphorical shadow on an eponymous plaza at San Francisco's ferry terminal, but the working landscape he knew is gone from view.

Out of sight, traces of the shoreline's working past persist beneath high-rises and cafés. Yerba Buena Cove, San Francisco's original harbor, was its earliest center of gainful employment. Merchants, seamen, and the people who supported them operated from piers and boats moored or beached at the cove.[4] The Financial District has covered up the cove, but artifacts of maritime labor still come to light. From time to time, construction workers excavating the foundations of buildings for office workers unearth old ships buried under new land. Their discoveries give rise to jobs for scholars: the excavation, interpretation, and reconstruction endeavors of archaeologists who piece together stories from ruins. The effort to understand San Francisco's original landscape of work, where access to the bay was essential, emerges from the effort of building a new landscape of work where access to the bay is an amenity. The two places exist simultaneously, one on top of the other.

Old and new working landscapes come together at Fisherman's Wharf, too. On the water, work still means resource extraction. Since the nineteenth century San Francisco's fishing fleet has gone out each morning for the daily catch – and a seamen's chapel has blessed the enterprise. Fisheries have declined, but the fleet still catches herring, king salmon, albacore tuna, black cod, halibut, and crab.[5] Processed and sold along the pier, fresh fish makes its way into the leisure economy, where work means entertainment. Fisherman's Wharf meets the city in a row of restaurants where cooks, waiters, busboys, and cleaners prepare, serve, and tidy up meals for people who visit the edge of the bay for fun: the landscape of work and the landscape of play come together in plates of Dungeness crab and bowls of cioppino.[6] But diners don't see most of the people responsible for their meals. Doors separate kitchens from dining rooms, and the restaurant buildings hide views of the fleet and the pier. Labor takes place behind the scenes.

The shoreline's last remaining industrial landscape, Potrero Point, always lay at San Francisco's margins. Located to keep the nuisances of factories and foundries away from

---

4 Delgado, *Gold Rush Port.*
5 Information about the catch comes from the website of the San Francisco Community Fishing Association. Denis Cuff discussed the problem of declining fisheries in two articles in San Jose's *Mercury News*: "Herring Harvest: Inside the Last Commercial Fishery in San Francisco Bay" and "Bay Area Commercial Fishing: Inside the Decline," 1 March 2013.
6 Cioppino is a fish stew with origins in San Francisco; its ingredients vary but always include fish, shellfish, tomatoes, and white wine.

the places most people went, it was a back-of-house counterpart to the commercial district downtown. Raw materials and manufactured goods could come and go by ship and train without bothering (or being bothered by) people who weren't directly involved. Potrero Point produced steel, sugar, ships, rope, barrels, mining equipment, and power. Now, though its shipyard still operates and its generating plant produces a third of San Francisco's electricity, the district has become a shadow of its former self. Just to the north, scientists carry out biotechnology research; to the west, designers and software developers have taken over old manufacturing buildings. Grittiness is giving way to the knowledge economy.

The view from San Francisco's shoreline still includes a working landscape, but it's on the other side of San Francisco Bay. Oakland became the bay's main port because it was big enough to accommodate container shipping. Longshoremen no longer haul break-bulk cargo from boats; instead, great cranes move containers between ships and the beds of trucks and railway cars. What was the work of many can now be done by a few. Maritime trade remains central to the urban economy, but it's separated from urban life. Cut off from the rest of Oakland by highways and rail lines, the port is a place unto itself.

Across the United States and the developed world, people who still work with their bodies have been pushed out of sight. At the edge of San Francisco Bay, they're behind construction hoardings, or at the far end of the pier, or in the factories on the south side of town, or at the port on the opposite shore. The last laborers in view work on the water: ships still need sailors to cross oceans and pilots to guide them through the Golden Gate and across the harbor.

Pilots work with their bodies and their minds. They sail at all hours and in the roughest weather. Time pressure is constant, clearances are tight, and conditions on the water change rapidly. The potential for disaster never disappears. Working as a pilot demands both conceptual knowledge and practical skill. Understanding navigational principles and tide tables isn't the same as steering a thousand-foot vessel through the ship channel.

Piloting is an old job, legally mandated and regulated since the earliest days of California's statehood. Pilots have guided ships to and from harbor since the nineteenth century, but continuity does not mean sameness. Technology has altered navigation's tools and techniques. Vessels have grown many times larger since the Gold Rush, and they travel under mechanical power rather than sail. The bay is different, too; neither its floor nor its edges match their nineteenth-century conditions. The longshoremen on the piers have been replaced by strollers and birdwatchers. Many of them will make use of the cargo arriving by ship, but few will know about the work – or the workers – required to deliver it to market. Today's pilots sail toward a shoreline their predecessors wouldn't recognize.

Play

In standard definitions, to play is to engage in an activity for amusement and without practical ends. The *Oxford English Dictionary* speculates that the word's origins connect to a Middle Dutch term meaning "to dance, leap for joy, rejoice, be glad."[7] All of those expressions of pleasure take place at the edge of San Francisco Bay. Most of the playing along shoreline engages more-than-human phenomena, from wind and waves to birds and flowers. Some playgrounds, like swimming and boating spots and San Francisco's two World's Fairs, were made to purpose. Others, like decommissioned military bases and abandoned jetties, were turned into parks as their previous functions grew obsolete. Even landscapes made for utility offer opportunities for delight.

The purpose-built playground of Aquatic Park emerged from a social mandate to put people to work. During the Great Depression, the federal government's Works Progress Administration commissioned unemployed artists, architects, and labourers to create a landscape for enjoying the shoreline. The play space they designed and built has become an iconic public room in San Francisco and on the bay. At Aquatic Park, play is physical. A curving pier extends from a constructed beach to make a sheltered cove for swimming, sailing, or rowing in a small boat. People who prefer to stay dry can walk to the pier's end for changing vistas of the bay and the city. Concrete bleachers overlook the cove so that spectators can watch the everyday theater of water games.

The bathhouse, built for the useful purpose of changing, combines practicality with spectacle; its shape evokes an Art Deco steamship, and imaginary sea creatures adorn its walls. The building has housed amusements beyond its original commission. In the 1930s, it served as an illegal gambling parlor; now it's a maritime museum where nostalgia transforms utilitarian objects into sources of delight.

Aquatic Park defined the public playground as a place to be in and on the water. San Francisco's two World's Fairs put forward a different notion: playground as urban spectacle. Composed of fantastic buildings and gardens, the fairs were scenographic distillations of a city. People came for pleasure, but their amusements centered on the celebration of business. At the first fair, the 1915 Panama–Pacific Exposition, eight of ten palaces devoted to cultural endeavors related to useful employment: Agriculture, Education, Food Products, Machinery, Manufactures, Mines and Metallurgy, Transportation, and Varied Industries. Only one souvenir of the spectacle remains: the Palace of Fine Arts. In its afterlife, the palace has served for both work and play. At various moments,

---

7 *Oxford English Dictionary*, s.v. "Play."

the plaster of Paris original housed tennis courts, a military motor pool, and a telephone distribution center. Reconstructed in concrete, the building became the Exploratorium, a museum that teaches science playfully.[8] After more than four decades, the museum moved across town; at present the palace stands empty in a city park. Like the ornamental ruins in an English landscape, it's a place for daydreams and assignations: a folly.

A quarter-century after the Panama–Pacific Exhibition closed, the Golden Gate International Exposition opened. It focused on the goods and commerce of the Pacific Rim, and its brilliantly illuminated buildings and gardens combined Moderne architectural fantasies with Asian and South American motifs.[9] The extravaganza occupied land made to be useful: the Works Progress Administration had built Treasure Island to create space for a new international airport. The fair closed in 1940. A year later, with the Second World War on the American horizon, Treasure Island became a naval base. Sailors replaced pleasure seekers.

Other places along the edge of the bay tell the same story in reverse. Decommissioned military installations constitute the country's first urban national park, the Golden Gate National Recreation Area. Visitors come for a kind of amusement not seen at the World's Fairs: contact with a landscape that has been relatively untouched by the city. Closed to civilians, the army bases that lined San Francisco's north shore acted as unplanned bastions against urban development; they protected ecosystems that the rest of the city had paved over. In the last decades of the twentieth century, as the environmental movement waxed and the Cold War waned, public consciousness about the value of time spent outside the urban fray intersected with public decisions to close military bases. The army gradually left San Francisco, and its lands became refuges for people as well as flora and fauna. Nature lovers replaced soldiers.

Like the army lands, Heron's Head grew accidentally into a playground for urban escapists; cultural neglect made it into a landscape suited to pursuits in nature. The abutment for a bridge that was never built became infrastructure for a voluntary marsh, and the marsh attracts birds. There are so many species that the park has its own handbook, *A Field Guide to 100 Birds of Heron's Head.*[10] Watching birds is a quiet but competitive pastime. Serious birders keep journals of all the species and specimens they've seen.

---

8 This history of the Palace of Fine Arts's uses appeared formerly on the website of the Exploratorium.
9 For a discussion of the fair's landscape and buildings see Anna Burrows, "The San Francisco Golden Gate Exhibition 1939–1940," available through the digital archive *A Treasury of World's Fair Art & Architecture.*
10 Bartley et al., *A Field Guide to 100 Birds of Heron's Head.*

When someone spots a rare bird, other people race to the site to get a look.[11] And the name of the park plays with words. It's a metaphor: from above, the shape of the abutment looks like the head of a heron. Heron's Head's pleasures derive from its wildness – and from the scarcity of such wildness at the edge of the bay. What's rare is special; what's special brings delight.

Delight emerges from what's unnecessary, too, like living in a houseboat at Mission Creek. The creek is the last vestige of Mission Bay, where shipyards, factories, and warehouses occupied the shoreline (and later, the new ground built on tidelands). Houseboats arrived as the working landscape declined. The fun of life on the water was amplified by the thrills of life at the margins of the city most people knew. Until the turn of the twenty-first century, the neighborhood's wharves and industrial buildings were punctuated by eccentric playgrounds: a golfers' driving range and an RV park. Since then, redevelopment has brought apartment buildings, grocery stores, biotech companies, and hospitals to Mission Bay.[12] Surrounded by contemporary San Francisco, the houseboats look charmingly impractical. They've been tethered to the systems of the city, but they stay afloat in spirit.

Houseboats are unnecessary and uncommon. Restaurants are unnecessary and ubiquitous. Dining out removes the obligations of mealtime: the ordinary activity of eating becomes play when someone else prepares the food and does the dishes. In the restaurants on Fisherman's Wharf, the taste of fresh fish is enhanced by salt air, a view of the water, and the arrival of dinner through the efforts of others: waiters and waitresses serve the meal, chefs and dishwashers cook and clean up, and fishermen sail from the pier to catch what's on the menu. Work backstage enables play at the table.

Sometimes necessities produce pleasures. When wind powered ships, sailing was a job. To carry cargo and passengers across the bay required expert crews with specialized knowledge, and long voyages were hardships. Struggle gave rise to beauty, though. The work of staying on course lent poetry to everyday language; even on dry land, people learn to give one another leeway or to take another tack. New technology made work into play. These days, cargo travels in diesel-powered ships, and sailing is a sport. The captains of the small craft that ply the bay wrestle with the wind for fun. The marina

---

11 Jonathan Franzen offers a lovely description of birders' behavior in the essay "My Bird Problem," *The New Yorker*, 8 August 2005, 52.

12 Carol Lloyd's article "Still Afloat: Mission Creek's Houseboat Community Lives on in the Midst of Urban Development" discusses the history of the community; it appeared in the *San Francisco Chronicle*, 5 September 2011.

on San Francisco's north shore is a port at toy scale. A breakwater calms the waves; boats tie up at small piers; and yacht clubs stand in for warehouses. Rendered in miniature, maritime infrastructure produces space for recreation.

In the steep hills above the bay, small-scale infrastructure creates pleasure grounds where streets stop and rights-of-way carry through as stairs. The love children of precipitous slopes and a strict grid, San Francisco's stairways delight people who prefer beauty to convenience. The climb is never required: the next passable street is only a block away. Stairways break the strict decorum of San Francisco's streets. Narrow and overgrown, they're like secret gardens; because they're so steep, the cottages on either side can't follow the rules of party-wall construction. Stairs turn familiar patterns into unfamiliar spaces, and that surprise changes the trudge uphill into an escape from the city's usual scenery. With their rigorous ascents, they're playgrounds for athletes in training. Secluded from the chance encounters of busy sidewalks, they're playgrounds for lovers and daydreamers.

Daydreams flourish at the edge of the bay, too. They thrive on the play of light on water. Reflections have their own way of making the familiar slightly strange. Even the most utilitarian scenes look different – and beautiful – when they're pictured on the moving surface of the water. The workaday world becomes special, and the magic of its transformation is cause for rejoicing.

Keywords 6

Time

Standard dictionaries define time as an abstraction, the continuum in which change transpires. But as we live from day to day, time becomes embodied. We register the passage of those days (and weeks, months, years, and decades) because we observe change: on the clock, in ourselves, in one another, and in the landscape. Landscapes change at different scales of time. They vary cyclically with the Earth and Moon, and as cycles accumulate, they evolve from one state into another. Transformation comes from processes beyond people's control –like the rise and fall of tides – and through human action – like the construction of a new ground plane (and a new city) higher than the high tide at San Francisco Bay.

In concert patter before the song "Who Knows Where the Time Goes?" Nina Simone told her audience,

> Sometime in your life, you will have occasion to say, "What is this thing called time?" …Where does it go? What does it do? Most of all, is it alive?[1]

All of those questions apply at the edge of the bay, where time is at once mysterious and measurable. How do people mark time's passage? What shifts do they read? What histories do they forget? And as the landscape changes, where and how do traces of the past remain alive in the present?

Interval

An interval is a distinct measure or length between two points in time. Clocks measure time in seconds, minutes, and hours; calendars count in days, weeks, months, and years. Landscape intervals occur on different scales and indices. Some recur in cycles: days,

---

1 Ms Simone's musings were recorded on her live album, *Black Gold* (1970). The song "Who Knows Where the Time Goes?" was written by Sandy Denny.

months, seasons. Some accumulate in series: years, lifetimes, generations, ages, epochs. Sometimes people measure change in moments, singular events that stand out from the ordinary flow of days, months, years, and decades.

At the edge of San Francisco Bay, people count days and months by the tides and the phases of the Moon. Even though the construction of new land keeps tides off shore, people on the water still use them to measure time. Kayakers see the pilings below piers emerge and disappear over the course of a day, and pilots perceive the tides in their ships' changing clearances. The Moon tells its story on land and water. As it waxes and wanes, anyone with a view of the sky can count the months. Erasing the tidelands hasn't obscured all signs of time and tide.

The bay's salinity measures time, too: it tracks the seasons. The salt wedge where ocean water and river water meet has always moved inland during California's dry summer and autumn; in winter and spring, when rain falls and snow melts, it has always shifted back toward the Golden Gate. Water diversions from rivers to aqueducts have changed the pattern. Salt migrates upstream sooner and longer than it used to, and freshwater plants and animals suffer the consequences. Human intervention has disrupted the time cycles that regulate more-than-human life.

Obsessed by progress, the culture at the edge of San Francisco Bay tends to care less about time's recurring cycles than its forward movement. From that point of view, the landscape looks like a physical register of sequential events. The bottom of the bay records history on a vertical axis: the top layer of mud is the most recent. At Hunters Point Naval Shipyard, mud provides a timeline of wrongdoing. For decades, the navy dumped toxic chemicals at the shipyard, and they settled on the bay floor. After Superfund required remediation, adjudicators needed to know when the pollution occurred. Mud cores that revealed the sequence of chemical deposition provided data for the reconstruction of events. The timeline in the mud preserved a history of human activity even in a place where people didn't go themselves.

Sediment wrote more-than-human history when it built the marsh at Heron's Head. Like the sediment at Hunters Point, it accumulated undetected; though it lay above water, it was out of people's sight. Its accretion produced two timelines. One was spatial. The constructed landmass of the jetty widened as sediment piled up against it and marsh plants stabilized soil. The other was ecological. Over forty years, the jetty's bare rock has given rise to habitat for more and more diverse flora and fauna.[2] The unintended con-

---

2 This process, in which living systems emerge from non-living material, is called primary succession.

sequences of longshore drift make it possible to measure time by changes in space – and in complexity.

Change can only be gauged against known points of beginning; at Heron's Head, ecological diversity emerged from bare riprap and a marsh grew out from the fixed edge of a jetty. Mission Rock, a drowned bit of the Coast Ranges, has served as an index of change for San Francisco's shoreline. In the middle of the nineteenth century, the rock lay a mile offshore from the coast of Mission Bay. The boundary between land and water moved east as people filled in the bay's shallows. New land crept toward Mission Rock for decades, and then, after the Second World War, it leapt eastward. By the early 1950s, the rock had been subsumed by the construction of Pier 50. Someone who spent his working life on the waterfront could watch the shoreline's leading edge describe a timeline, increment by increment.

Changes in the landscape can change the time needed to cover the same distance; it's faster to drive (or even walk) across paved streets to the end of Pier 50 than it would have been to sail to Mission Rock. If time is money, speed has value. San Francisco's street grid makes the hills above the edge of the bay slow going. A person who travels over Russian Hill on Broadway faces a steep, slow climb and a precipitous descent. The trip is hard on clutches, brakes, and drivers. Going under the hill, through the level route of the Broadway Tunnel, the ride takes a fraction of the time required on the surface. The faster, easier trip brings the western half of the city closer to the bay. It saves time.[3]

Planes save time, too. In the 1930s, when Pan American Airways began trans-Pacific service from Treasure Island to Manila, the voyage by steamship took almost three weeks. Pan Am's seaplanes made the trip in sixty hours spread over six days.[4] Lines through air are shorter than lines through water, and they keep getting shorter. Today, flights from San Francisco to Manila last 14 hours and 27 minutes, plus takeoff and landing. Time becomes a measure of distance: we say that San Francisco is about fifteen hours from Manila.

Time measures distance at another scale in the sounding of San Francisco Bay. Since the 1920s, the US government has used SONAR to measure the bay floor. Given the speed of sound (roughly 1,500 meters per second through seawater) and the depth of San Francisco Bay (just over 40 feet on average, 360 feet at its lowest), sound renders distance in an instant.[5] The interval of measurement is so short that it's perceived as a discrete moment.

---

3 The Broadway Tunnel was part of a comprehensive freeway plan for San Francisco. The 1948 scheme is laid out in San Francisco Department of City Planning, *Progress*. A drawing of the city's fast new roads is available online as Plate 8 of "[San Francisco] Comprehensive Trafficways Plan" on the website of the David Rumsey Historical Map Collection.
4 "Transport: Transpacific," *Time Magazine*, 2 December 1935.
5 University of Rhode Island and Inner Space Center, "How Fast Does Sound Travel?," *Discovery of Sound in the Sea*.

Moments enter people's consciousness as singular events that stand out from ordinary time. Measuring time in days and seasons means reading change in cycles. Measuring time over years and decades means reading change in serial accumulations. Measuring time in moments means reading rapid, concentrated change. Like comets or jets, moments have long tails. They leave persistent traces.

Some moments in the history of the bay can be pinpointed to the minute. At 8:30 a.m. on 7 November 2007, the *Cosco Busan*, a container ship leaving the Port of Oakland, hit one of the towers of the Bay Bridge and punctured its fuel tank. The consequences unfolded at different scales of time. Over hours, oil leaked out of the tank. Over days, 58,000 gallons of oil spread across the bay and beyond the Golden Gate. Over weeks, rescue workers collected and treated nearly three thousand oiled birds. Over years, herring in the bay suffered developmental harm and an elevated death rate. A moment instigated by a single person changed animal habitat in and around San Francisco Bay dramatically and for the long term.

At another pinpoint in time, 5:04 pm on 17 October 1989, forces beyond people's control changed human habitat at the edge of the bay in equally dramatic ways. The Loma Prieta earthquake lasted only fifteen seconds, but it transformed San Francisco's waterfront: it returned spaces that had been out of bounds to the everyday landscape of the city. The Embarcadero Freeway was dismantled because of earthquake damage, and for the first time in thirty years, people on the streets of the Financial District could see San Francisco Bay. Vulnerable to further damage, the elevated part of Doyle Drive was replaced by a road below grade. Loma Prieta catalyzed change in circumstances that had evolved over time: the decline of the working waterfront made the shoreline available as an urban amenity, and the army's departure from the Presidio offered up the base as a park. Now a palm-lined boulevard runs along the Embarcadero, and a planted deck over Doyle Drive will connect the Presidio to the bay. The consequences of a moment have recast infrastructure as public space.

At San Francisco's World's Fairs, momentary public spaces provided reasons to build infrastructure. Both World's Fairs entailed the construction of significant tracts of land: 196 acres for 1915 and more than 430 acres for 1939. After the parties ended, the fairgrounds became part of the everyday city. Land made for the Panama–Pacific International Exposition became the Marina District. The Golden Gate International Exposition's grounds became a naval base; after the base closed, San Francisco took the land back for civilian redevelopment. The Palace of Fine Arts and Treasure Island's Administration Building stand out as souvenirs of spectacle, but individual structures matter less than the long-term claiming of land from the bay. The moments of the fairs shaped long-term patterns of urban development.

In between the World's Fairs, during the domestic crisis of the Great Depression, the US government defined the political moment of the New Deal. That interval of social change transformed the landscape of San Francisco Bay. The New Deal provided public funds to build public places. On San Francisco's north shore, a bathhouse, a beach, bleachers, and a curving pier defined a cove for swimmers and small boats: an aquatic park. Treasure Island provided the grounds for the 1939 World's Fair and served as a naval base. The Bay Bridge has had the longest tail of all the New Deal projects. Like the Broadway Tunnel, it changed the relationship between time and space: it made the voyage between San Francisco and the East Bay into a quick drive, and that shortcut turned the city into a metropolis.

The New Deal defined a decade. Loma Prieta took fifteen seconds. Moments vary in their duration, but they share an essential characteristic: they're finite intervals of time that initiate profound change in the landscape. They separate *before* from *after*.

Souvenir

General dictionaries define souvenirs as things that prompt memory; they're vestiges and reminders of other times. William Faulkner wrote, "The past is never dead. It isn't even past."[6] Landscapes prove his point.[7] They change, but they always contain traces of their previous states: souvenirs. At the edge of San Francisco Bay, some souvenirs announce their histories: places like Fort Point and the Palace of Fine Arts maintain their forms and identities even though their meanings and circumstances have evolved. Other artifacts of the past, like shipwrecks on the bay floor and the bedrock that supports the towers of the Bay Bridge, lie hidden beneath the landscape's surface – and below the level of ordinary awareness. Knowing that the past remains alive reminds us that landscapes evolve in continuous arcs. Deciphering its manifestations changes the way we read the present, and that colors our ideas about what might be next.

---

6 Faulkner, *Requiem for a Nun*, 73.

7 Because of the persistent traces of the past, geomorphologists think of landscape as a palimpsest, an accretion of overlaid and interacting layers comparable to a parchment text that remains legible despite erasure and overwriting. Goudie and Viles, *Landscapes and Geomorphology*. In *Los Angeles: The Architecture of Four Ecologies*, Banham used the same metaphor in his discussion of the city's transportation networks; there, freeways occupy the spaces previously defined by colonial roads, railways, and inter-urban streetcars.

Some souvenirs are objects. From time to time, the scouring action of storms brings up nineteenth-century shipwrecks from the bay floor. The wrecks recall San Francisco's maritime origins: the city owed its existence to a harbor that connected California's interior riches to the rest of the world. Beyond that, the lost ships are artifacts of risk and reward. People braved the hazards of a voyage to San Francisco for the chance to acquire great wealth in a short time. The boats that come to light are cataloged and entered in public records, but the Gold Rush left behind less tangible traces, too. San Francisco's economy no longer depends on the sea, but the culture of risk and reward is alive and well. Technology has made the city a boomtown again.

Processes can be souvenirs, too. The east face of Telegraph Hill is still wearing away because of quarrying that ended more than a century ago. From the Gold Rush to the early twentieth century, San Franciscans mined the slope for ballast and construction materials. They instigated a chain of events they couldn't control. Blasting made deep cracks that destroyed the hill's structure. Quarries left cliffs so steep that plants couldn't take root. Water eroded the bare surfaces, and rocks and soil began to tumble to the bottom of the hill. Latter-day responses to the instability, retaining walls and nets contain the slope and its debris.

To contain a natural process is not to stop it. Before San Francisco was a city, water traveled overland from San Bruno Mountain and Mount Davidson to the bay; it ran though Islais Creek. When people built roads through the creek's valley, they moved its channel into pipes and culverts. The engineered drainage system traces the creek's branches and trunk; out of sight but audible through the grates of storm drains, water still flows along its old route. Climate change will bring more rain than the pipes can hold, and sooner or later, the creek will break through its confines underground. The stream will return to the surface, and the past will be present again.

Another, older river course runs beneath San Francisco Bay. During the last Ice Age, the deep channel between Carquinez Strait and the Golden Gate carried water from the Sierra Nevada mountains through a valley in the Coast Ranges. Melting glaciers turned the valley into a bay, and the river was drowned. The ancient river's tributaries are still eroding the Sierra Nevada's slopes; they still bring traces of the mountains to the bay. In the nineteenth century, they carried mercury, too.

Hydraulic mining was banned in the 1880s, but metamorphosis preserves a souvenir: mercury persists in the watershed and the bay – and in their inhabitants. *Now* connects to *then* through a series of material transformations. Water eroded the hills; mercury dissolved the gold; rivers carried the mercury; bacteria turned an element into a compound;

one creature ate (and still eats) another. Like children playing telephone, miners' ghosts whisper across time to people fishing at the edge of the bay.

Water cannons still echo in the high-rises of the Financial District, too, though more abstractly: the gold mines of the nineteenth century produced the urban canyons of the twenty-first. The Gold Rush turned a colonial outpost into an instant city – and a parking place for wealth. Banks founded with gold made San Francisco the financial center of the American west coast; now the city's banks exert influence across the country. The Financial District's glittering towers represent transmuted wealth from the mines. Gold became money; money became credit; credit increased the wealth held by banks; and banks expressed their wealth through buildings that signify power and prestige.

Sometimes the past touches the present directly, without abstraction or translation. A car that crosses the Bay Bridge today connects to more than one kind of history; its weight moves through souvenirs of different ages. The bridge's original spans are remnants of the New Deal. Its steel components are technological artifacts of the nineteenth century, when foundries began to produce iron and carbon alloys in large quantities. Its towers rise from concrete foundations, and its Center Anchorage contains more concrete than the Empire State Building. The concrete reaches back two thousand years (Vitruvius described its use in classical Rome), and it rests on rock formed three or four million years ago. Bedrock carries the weight of the cars – and their drivers.

Before the Bay Bridge meets its Rincon Hill anchorage, it hangs suspended over the Embarcadero. The shadow it casts is the souvenir of an earlier shoreline; the bridge remains aloft because the built edge of the bay can't support its structure. The shadow on the new land is a reminder of the past and a premonition of the future. As glaciers melt and sea level rises, San Francisco Bay will reclaim the territory it lost to the city. The old land's scalloped coves will come back into view, though not as they were before. Landscape detectives will find traces of the line people drew between land and water. They'll read its remnants as souvenirs of now.

A Field Guide to the Edge of the Bay

This field guide documents artifacts, places, and phenomena a person encounters along the length of San Francisco's edge with San Francisco Bay. Examining the shoreline's hybrid landscape place by place is a way to understand its parts, and many of the guide's forty-eight entries call attention to something that might otherwise go unnoticed. Ordered by location, the entries trace an eleven-mile route from Fort Point, at the Golden Gate, to Hunters Point, near the city's southern border. The linear map that follows this introduction shows the route and identifies each field entry's place on it. Like standard field guides, *Bay Lexicon* uses images and text to help readers name, classify, and interpret elements of the physical environment. Its field entries are designed to build visual and verbal vocabulary for the landscape.

Each entry begins with a documentary drawing of its subject – and a question meant to prompt thought about what lies behind the scene. The drawings articulate and argue for ideas in varied ways. Their framing and composition edits extraneous information, so each drawing brings attention to what's most important in its scene. To show conditions and relationships beneath or within what's visible, some drawings combine images in perspective with analytical conventions such as cross-section. Other drawings use familiar symbols (for instance, an old-fashioned figure of the wind or an image of a ruler) to depict invisible forces and dynamics (for instance, the energy that motivates waves or the gradual rising of the tide). The drawings juxtapose different scales to suggest the conjunction of spaces and times that might seem remote from each other. They include human figures to show us our own place in the landscape.

Every documentary drawing in the field guide becomes the anchor for layers of annotation and commentary: a reference to its location; the names and definitions of its elements; a question about what's pictured; a short essay that meditates on answers; relevant citations; and keywords that connect the subject to broad themes about the edge of the bay. The entries in the field guide are organized spatially: they occur in series as points on a map. The keywords associated with each entry provide an alternative organization; they classify the entry in relation to places and subjects that may not be proximate. Field entries appear in relation to more than one keyword because the situations they document have plural meanings and implications.

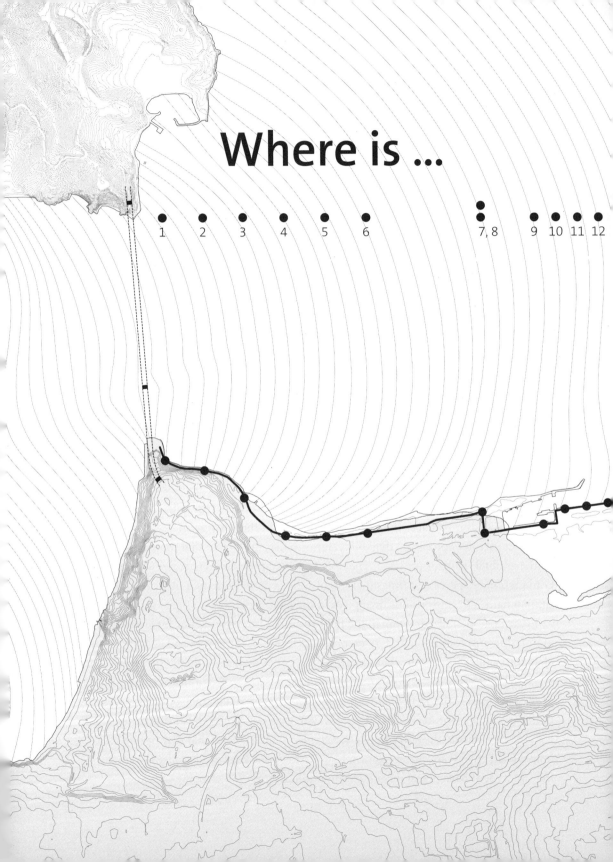

Where is ...

1   2   3   4   5   6   7, 8   9   10   11   12

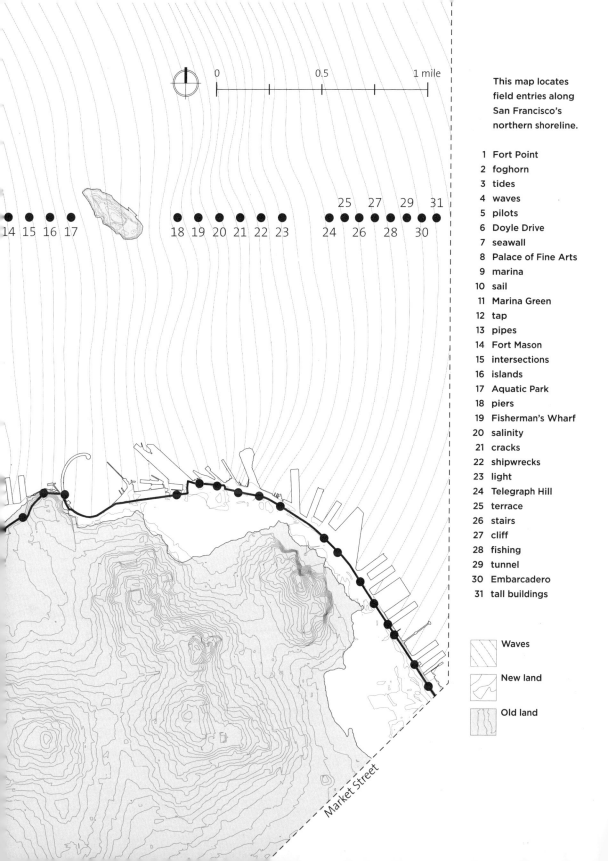

This map locates
field entries along
San Francisco's
northern shoreline.

1 Fort Point
2 foghorn
3 tides
4 waves
5 pilots
6 Doyle Drive
7 seawall
8 Palace of Fine Arts
9 marina
10 sail
11 Marina Green
12 tap
13 pipes
14 Fort Mason
15 intersections
16 islands
17 Aquatic Park
18 piers
19 Fisherman's Wharf
20 salinity
21 cracks
22 shipwrecks
23 light
24 Telegraph Hill
25 terrace
26 stairs
27 cliff
28 fishing
29 tunnel
30 Embarcadero
31 tall buildings

0   0.5   1 mile

14 15 16 17

25   27   29   31

18 19 20 21 22 23   24 26 28 30

Waves

New land

Old land

Market Street

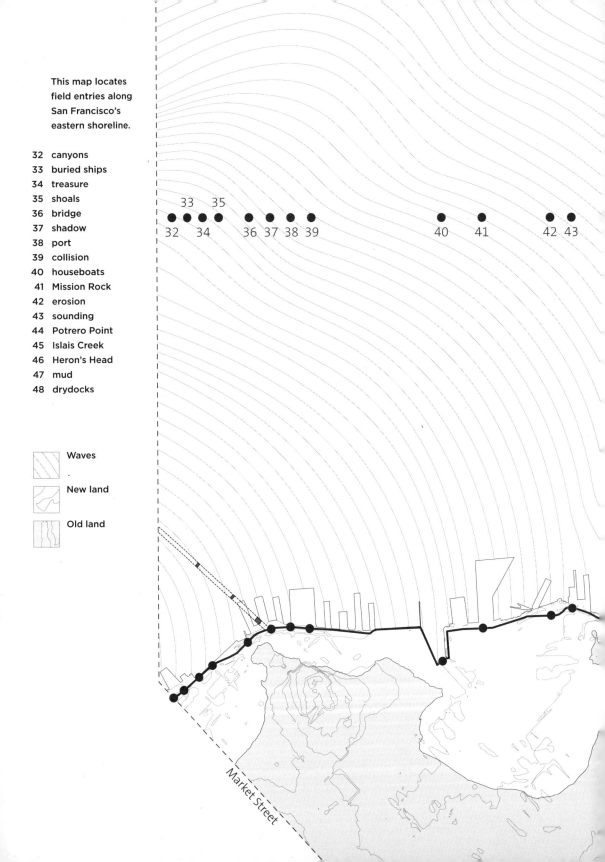

This map locates field entries along San Francisco's eastern shoreline.

Waves

New land

Old land

32 33 34 35 36 37 38 39   40   41   42 43

Market Street

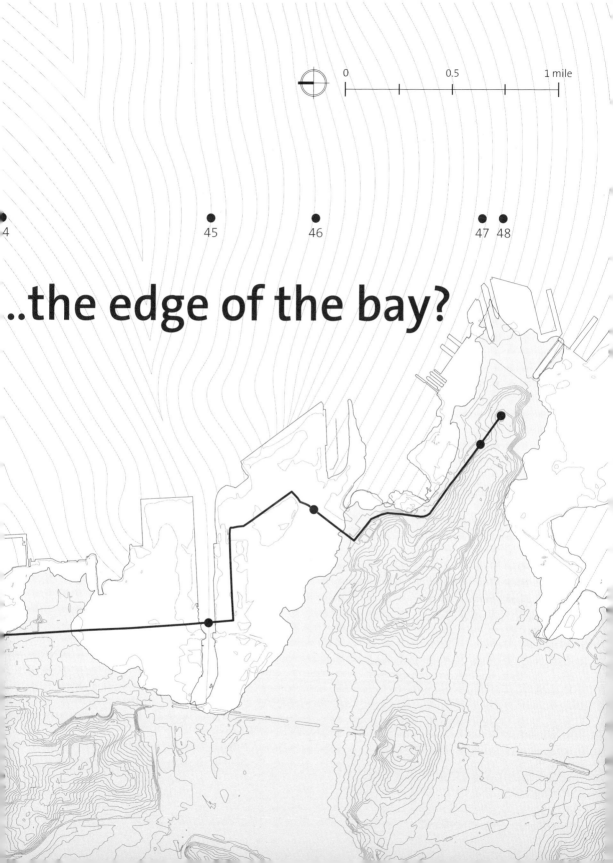

..the edge of the bay?

What does Fort Point guard?

a. strait: a narrow channel, defined by promontories on either side and usually navigable, that connects significant bodies of water.

b. bay: a water body in open connection to the sea but sheltered on most sides by land.

c. interior: the inland part of a region. The interior of California comprises the Central Valley and the Sierra Nevada.

1 Fort Point

- - - - - - - - - - - - - - -

Fort Point watches over the Golden Gate. It was built to guard the strait and everything beyond: the harbor, the city, and the interior of California. San Francisco Bay is the single maritime point of access to the Central Valley and the Sierra Nevada. When the US Army undertook the fort's construction, the bay offered the only route to gold in the mountains.

The Golden Gate's strategic importance was clear even before gold was discovered. The Spanish established a garrison at the Presidio, just inside the strait, in 1776, and they built the first fort on the point in 1794. The United States took possession of California in 1848, the year the Gold Rush made San Francisco Bay the most valuable harbor on the continent. In 1853, the army broke ground for a massive installation at Fort Point. Conceived as part of a battery of military fortifications to defend the bay against foreign and Confederate invaders, Fort Point was finished in 1861. By the turn of the twentieth century, its artillery capacity had been surpassed by new batteries at the Presidio. The fort fell into intermittent use and decline even though the bay's military importance increased: the Pacific theaters of the Spanish-American War, the Second World War, the Korean War, and the Vietnam War filled the landscape with army and navy installations.

Our swords are not yet plowshares, but the army has left San Francisco Bay. Today, both sides of the Golden Gate belong to a national recreation area, and Fort Point is a museum.*

Keywords: Defense, Land, Play

---

* The drawing of Fort Point is based on an 1868 photograph of the Presidio, "Fort Point from the South," located on the website of the National Park Service.

Why do foghorns sound?

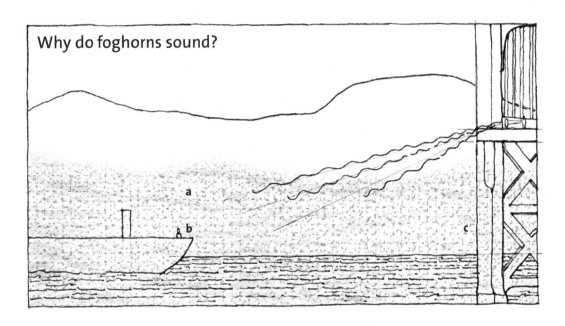

a. fog: water vapor condensed in a mass just above the ground.
b. pilot: a local navigation expert who boards a ship to guide it safely into or out of port.
c. hazard: a source of danger. Unseen hazards pose the greatest risks.

2 Foghorn

The low fog that rolls into San Francisco Bay from the Pacific hides everything, even the orange towers of the Golden Gate Bridge. Ship traffic through the bay is too heavy – and the fog too frequent – to wait for better weather, so foghorns on the bridge mitigate the hazards of limited visibility. They let hearing stand in for sight.

The foghorns are started by hand. Day and night, their operator watches for low fog from the bridge deck. When he sees it approaching, he pulls a toggle switch and the horns go on. Three horns in the middle of the span sound as two tones. Two horns at the south tower sound as a single tone, lower in register than the mid-span set and at a different interval. They spell out a code that tells a pilot where he is even when the bridge has disappeared from view. Ships heading into the bay steer between the horns; ships heading out to sea stay north of the horns at mid-span. When the fog clears and the foghorn operator can see Lands End and Point Bonita, he pulls the toggle to off and the horns fall silent.

On average, the foghorns sound for two and a half hours a day. In summer's foggy weather, they stay on for days at a time. Their signal constitutes a wordless greeting (or farewell) from operator to pilot.*

Keywords: Infrastructure, Navigation, Physics

---

* The Golden Gate Bridge Highway & Transportation District's website offers an explanation of operating procedures – and the chance to hear the sound of the foghorn. For further impressions of the fog and its effects on the city, see Andy Black and Sam Green, *A Cinematic Study of Fog in San Francisco*, 2013.

What changes the tide, and what does the tide change?

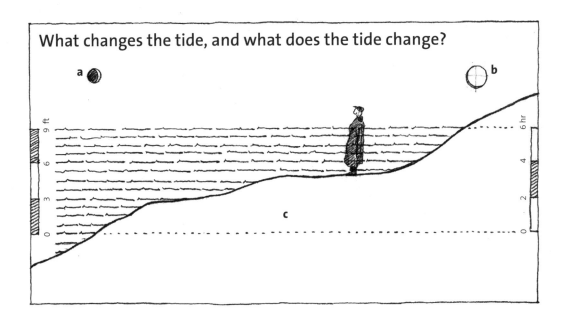

a. Moon: Earth's natural satellite. As the Moon orbits the Earth, its gravitational pull creates tides. High tides occur when the Moon is closest to and farthest from the bay.
b. Sun: the star around which the Earth orbits. At new and full moons, the Sun, Moon, and Earth are all aligned. The Sun's gravitational pull on the sea is added to the Moon's, and the difference between high and low tides is at its greatest. At quarter moons, the Sun and the Moon are at right angles. Their pulls do not add up, and the difference between high and low tides is at its lowest.
c. tidelands: places that are submerged at high tide and exposed at low tide.

3 Tides

Tides change because of gravity. The relative positions of the Sun and the Moon and their varying distances from the Earth make the level of water in the sea rise or allow it to fall.

When tides are high, the Pacific Ocean pushes into San Francisco Bay; when they are low, it retreats. Back and forth, tides change the boundary between the bay and the city every day, twice a day. Until 1851, this moving edge meant that land along the shore could not be owned. Then the potential value of property trumped ambiguity. A new federal law allowed the sale of tidelands, and they disappeared behind seawalls and under constructed ground.* Ideas changed reality: a social compact that defined land as a commodity fixed the shoreline and produced terrain high enough to stay dry. At this built edge, tides no longer swallow land. Their flux can only be measured vertically, against seawalls and pilings.

Where the new land ends, the story is different. Tides change a walk along the beach or through a marsh. They change the distance from the bottoms of boats to the bay floor and from the tops of stacks and masts to the spans of bridges. They change the chemistry of the water: when they flow, they bring salt into the bay, and when they ebb, they carry it away.

Keywords: Infrastructure, Interval, Physics, Water

---

* The Arkansas Swamp Lands Act of 1850, which gave the states title to all swamp and overflowed lands, made tidelands available for reclamation. California received title to more than two million acres; a series of state laws authorized their sale and reclamation. For a detailed account of this legislation and its consequences, see Booker, *Down by the Bay:* 44–68, 158; and Dow, "Bay Fill in San Francisco," 4–18.

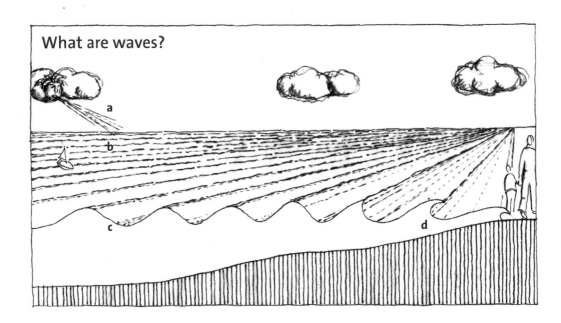

What are waves?

a. **wind:** the natural movement of air across water and land.

b. **fetch:** the expanse of water over which wind blows.

c. **swell:** a wave that travels across open water.

d. **breaker:** a wave that strikes the shore.

4 Waves

Waves move energy through water. They begin with the uneven distribution of heat from the Sun, which makes some parts of the Earth's surface hotter than others. The air above hot places rises; when cooler air nearby rushes to take its place, the wind blows in. Wind moving across water drags it forward, but not very far. Gravity pulls the water down almost immediately, and the force of its fall pushes what's below up to the surface. Each drop of water is carried in a circle, and together, the circular movements make a wave. The top of the wave is its crest. The bottom is its trough.

The longer and harder the wind blows and the greater its fetch, the bigger the waves it creates. The farther the waves move from their source, the larger and more regular they become. When they travel across the open ocean, they are called swells. When they hit the coast, they are called breakers. Their troughs slow down, held back by the shallow sea floor, but their crests keep going. Water piles up at the top of the wave, and eventually it topples onto the shore. Breakers land differently on different slopes. Some spill onto the beach, some plunge, some surge, and some collapse.

The swells that arrive at the Golden Gate have come from as far away as the Indian Ocean, but they do not survive the strait: they are dispersed as the enter the bay. The waves that break along the San Francisco shoreline are products of the local wind.

Keywords: Physics, Water

Who steers ships into harbor?

a. pilot: a local navigation expert who boards a ship to guide it safely into or out of port. Bar pilots are trained to navigate the shoals and sandbars that often lie near coastal harbors.

b. tugboat: a small, strong, sturdy boat that tows and pushes larger vessels through conditions they cannot navigate without aid.

5 Pilots

Maritime trade generates billions of dollars a year in and around San Francisco, and ship traffic on the bay is constant. Huge vessels travel to and from four local ports – San Francisco, Oakland, Richmond, and Redwood City – and two ports farther east – Stockton and Sacramento. Cargos vary. Tankers carry oil; bulkers move grain and ore; container ships transport manufactured goods; cruise ships convey passengers.

Steering a ship through the Golden Gate and across San Francisco Bay is like threading a needle. A great sandbar lies just outside the strait, the shipping channel is narrow, and the biggest vessels have only a few feet to clear the bridge spans and the channel floor. A stranger could never manage the journey. San Francisco's bar pilots steer all ships sailing between a point eleven miles west of the Golden Gate and their port berths. The pilots know the bay by heart. Their work is full of risk, and there is no margin for error. They schedule ships to sail with the tides, even in rough weather and heavy fog. Maritime choreographers, they direct the tugboats whose weight and counterweight steer and slow the enormous mass of ships nearly a thousand feet long.

More than four thousand ships face the hazards of San Francisco Bay every year. The bar pilots are safeguards against catastrophe.[*]

Keywords: Infrastructure, Navigation, Physics, Work

----

[*] This entry is based on an interview with Captain Drew Aune of the San Francisco Bar Pilots; the conversation took place aboard a pilot boat sailing from Pier 9 to the Golden Gate Bridge, 27 June 2012. Statistics about maritime volume and economic value are from the website of the San Francisco Bar Pilots.

What did the bridge cross?

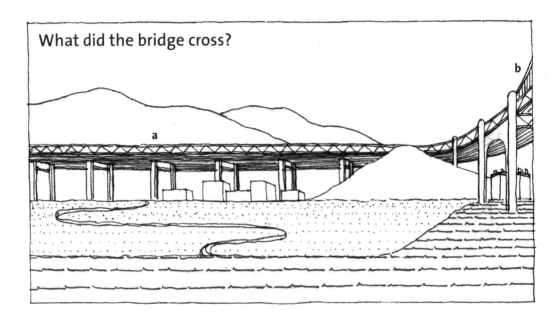

a.   viaduct: a series of spans that carries a roadway over low ground or across a valley. The word comes from Latin: *via* means way, and *ducere* means to bring or to lead.

b.   bridge: a structure that carries a roadway across a significant topographic gap like a strait or a river. Bridges usually have longer spans than viaducts. The word's origins are Anglo-Saxon, and it has cognates in German, Dutch, and Danish.

6 Doyle Drive

The original route between Marin County and San Francisco was designed to make two crossings, the Golden Gate and the Presidio. The bedrock anchorage of the Golden Gate Bridge made a narrow joint between the southern span and the high viaduct of its long tail, Doyle Drive. The roadway, elevated on piers that matched the bridge, continued seamlessly over Cavalry Valley, past the National Cemetery, and along Crissy Field. It finally touched ground behind the Palace of Fine Arts and joined the city grid at the intersection of Lombard and Broderick Streets, two blocks east of the Presidio's main gate.

A concrete line that connected the bridge to the city and separated the hills from the bay, Doyle Drive was built to enforce a ritual division: the boundary between military and civilian life. Until it was decommissioned in the 1990s, the Presidio was *terra incognita* inside city limits. The Department of War and the army's Ninth Corps Area[*] granted right of way for the bridge and its approach only on two conditions: there could be no intersections with base roads and no interference with military activities. Travelers across the Golden Gate remained suspended over land just as they had been suspended over water.

Today, the Presidio is public space and Doyle Drive is a memory. Its replacement has erased the history of separate spheres: shore and hills, fort and city. Times have changed, and so has the rhetoric of the road.

Keywords: Defense, Interval, Play

---

[*] When the Golden Gate Bridge and Doyle Drive were built, the Presidio fell under the jurisdiction of the Department of War (later called the Department of Defense); from 1920 to 1942, the base was the headquarters of the army's Ninth Corps Area. Thompson and Woodbridge, *Presidio of San Francisco.*

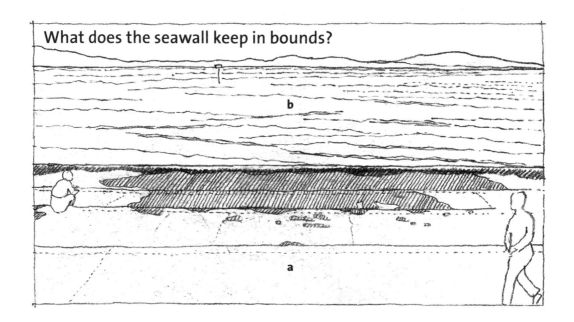

What does the seawall keep in bounds?

a.   filled land: new ground constructed along the shore by placing rubble and sand in marsh and tidelands.

b.   waves: ridges that travel along and through the surface of water. This disturbance marks the transfer of energy from one region of a water body to another but does not redistribute the water permanently.

7 Seawall

San Francisco's seawall draws a line between land and water. Before its construction, that border was ambiguous. The shore was marshy. The land was low and wet, and creeks and channels rose and fell with the rain and the tides. The seawall looks definite until high tide pushes waves up its shallow steps. Then the bay mocks the idea of a fixed boundary.

The oldest seawalls along the bay are as old as the city. Built to make a fortified edge for filled land, they extended the shoreline into deep water. They were infrastructure for shipping and for speculation: boats could tie up more easily, and the new ground was subdivided and sold.* Seawalls contain all of the places built out from San Francisco's once scalloped coast. They were constructed section by section over decades, part of a series of tactics to make land habitable and profitable. Their builders did not anticipate the climate emergency. This century's sea level rise demands their renewal.

San Francisco's seawall extends almost continuously from the Marina District to Hunter's Point. Most of it is hidden under piers, out of sight and out of mind. Only at the steps does it announce itself as the city's physical – and ideological – front line.

Keywords: Commerce, Defense, Infrastructure, Land, Water

---

* James P. Delgado discusses the initial filling of the shoreline in "Development of the Gold Rush Waterfront," in *Gold Rush Port*, 51–90.

What's constructed?

a. palace: a temporary but elaborate hall constructed to display products, in this case fine arts, at world's fairs.

b. lagoon: a shallow, calm body of water separated from the sea by sandbars or reefs, or here, by filled land.

c. filled land: new ground constructed along the shore by placing rubble and sand in marsh and tidelands.

d. recollection: a process of memory; the retrieval of something from the past.

8 Palace of Fine Arts

The Palace of Fine Arts and its surroundings are a fantastic construction, an invented world built from the rubble of the Great Earthquake and Fire of 1906. After the catastrophe, the marshlands and mudflats on the northern edge of San Francisco became a dumping ground for debris. Nine years later, that detritus was transformed into the stage for a world's fair, the Panama–Pacific International Exposition.* Designed to conjure exotic spectacles, the exposition's pavilions and palaces comprised a dream city, an alter ego to the everyday world. It was an ephemeral display. The elaborate buildings were made of plaster of Paris, and when the fair ended in December 1915, they were demolished. Only the Palace of Fine Arts survived.

The history of the palace describes a series of illusions. A temporary structure on uncertain ground, the building was meant to evoke a temple in decay, and the lagoon was created to serve as its mirror. Over time the palace became the ruin it was intended to resemble, but it was not allowed to crumble. Instead it was torn down and reconstructed in concrete, a permanent material that still preserves its image of faded splendor.

In the construction of memory, recollection involves the retrieval of the past. The Palace of Fine Arts is a repository of lost moments. It was born from the rubble of an earthquake. It serves as a souvenir of the fair. It makes a momentary image permanent. It has become a monument, something for people to remember.

Keywords: Construction, Interval, Play

----

* The earthquake and fire of 1906 destroyed much of San Francisco, and the World's Fair was intended to demonstrate the city's recovery from disaster. See Benedict, *The Anthropology of World's Fairs*.

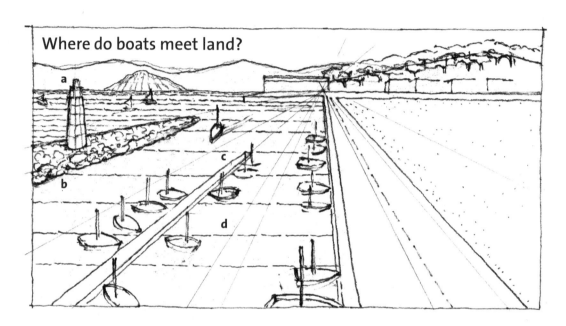

Where do boats meet land?

a. landmark: a fixed, recognizable feature that sailors use to identify their location.

b. breakwater: a structure that protects the coast from the full force of the waves.

c. landing: the place where a boat meets the shoreline. Landings are the threshold between land and sea.

d. marina: a harbor – or haven – for small pleasure boats.

9 Marina

Boats go between land and water. They exist so that people can extend their range beyond the shoreline.

In a marina, where small pleasure boats come to rest, the boundary between dry land and open water has layers. Lighthouses and other landmarks tell sailors they are approaching the shore. Breakwaters, long barriers built parallel to the coast, absorb the force of waves heading landward. Behind that, where the water is calm, landings provide places for boats to drop anchor and for sailors and passengers to come aboard and go ashore.

The marina on San Francisco's north shore replaced a marsh, a different kind of layered space between *terra firma* and the navigable bay. Built for the Panama–Pacific International Exposition, it was part of a significant extension of the city's seawall and landmass. In the 1920s, when the new land constructed for the fair was developed as housing, it lent its name to the neighborhood: the Marina District.

Keywords: Navigation, Play

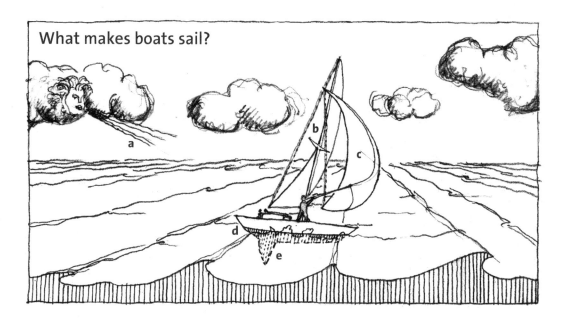

What makes boats sail?

a. wind: the natural movement of air across water and land.

b. spars: rigid beams used to support and maneuver sails. The mast, where the sail hangs, is vertical; the boom, which extends horizontally, is used to turn the sail.

c. sail: fabric sewn and fitted to a vessel in order to convert the wind's force into forward movement.

d. hull: the hollow, buoyant shell of a boat.

e. keel: a fin that extends from the bottom of a sailboat to give it lateral stability.

10 Sail

Sailing translates the forces of wind and water into forward motion.

Heading downwind, the process is straightforward. Wind rushing into a sail pushes a boat ahead. Heading upwind is more complicated. A boat heads into the wind at an angle, and its sail assumes a slight curve. The inside of the curve, on the windward side of the sail, is slightly shorter than the outside, on the leeward side. The wind moves faster across the sail's longer side than across its shorter side. Unequal wind speed creates unequal air pressure on either side of the sail, and the leeward face snaps windward to equalize the difference. This force – lift – begins to tip the hull, but water pushing against the keel acts as a counterbalance, and the boat is propelled ahead and slightly away from the wind. This drift off course is called leeway. To compensate, sailboats turn their bows, reversing their windward and leeward sides, and continue into the wind. Each change of direction is called a tack.

The language of sailing is all around us, even on land. When one strategy doesn't work, we take another tack. When we need a margin for error, we ask for a bit of leeway.

Keywords: Navigation, Physics, Play

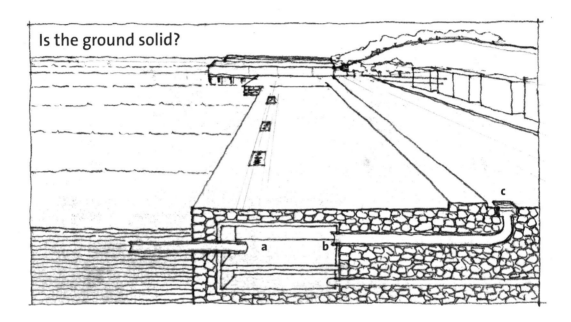

Is the ground solid?

a. vault: an underground chamber that collects water from the storm sewer system. Early sewers, made of masonry, had arched ceilings and walls; the vaulted cross-section gave the structure strength.
b. pipe: a cylindrical conduit that carries rain from the surface of the street into the sewer system.
c. water: rain that rushes from paved surfaces into drains, pipes, and vaults; groundwater that permeates filled land to the elevation of the bay.

11 Marina Green

Marina Green belongs to the surface of the city. A level plane built for the spectacle of the Panama–Pacific International Exposition, its lawn provides a carpet for everyday festivities – walks, kite launches, picnics. But the floor is also a roof. The lawn covers a hollow chamber: below the kite flyers and the dog walkers, an enormous sewer vault collects water from drains and gutters all over San Francisco.

Before the city was paved and plumbed, rain streamed down the hills in plain sight and met the tides in a marsh that ran along the bay's edge. Dense population made surface drainage inconvenient. Roadways and roofs shed water quickly, and fast-moving water created hazards. It eroded the ground; it backed up behind obstacles; it picked up debris; it carried suspended contaminants straight to the bay. Now it travels underground, sequestered in pipes and vaults. Streets and basements stay dry, and the captured water can be cleaned before its release.

Most of the time the sewers work well enough to be forgotten. Marina Green offers a clue to their invisible presence. The lawn is punctuated by metal plates that lift up for access to the vault below. Their surfaces are embossed with one word: WATER.*

Keywords: Construction, Play

---

* This drawing is based on a diagram I received from the San Francisco Public Utilities District.

What brings water to the tap?

a. river: a natural watercourse, flowing in a line from higher to lower ground.
b. delta: a landscape created by rivers as they approach the sea. In the California Delta, the Sacramento and San Joaquin Rivers split into a series of winding, slow-moving channels that converge at the Carquinez Strait and flow into San Francisco Bay.
c. dam: a barrier built across a river to create a reservoir.
d. aqueduct: a pipe or channel engineered to bring water to the city from far away.

12 Tap

- - - - - - - - -

San Francisco lives on borrowed water.

The city's watershed is defined twice: once by topography and once by engineering. The steep western slope of the Sierra Nevada sends rain and melting snow to San Francisco Bay. Water travels in streams and rivers down the Central Valley, through the California Delta, and past the Carquinez Strait, always moving toward the ocean. Since the 1930s, an aqueduct has carried some of that current on a different route. The Tuolumne River is captured behind Hetch Hetchy Dam and gradually released into pipes that run straight to San Francisco. Every spigot in the city is connected to the mountains.

The aqueduct is good and bad. It protects San Francisco from local scarcity, and it provides clean water, uncontaminated by the farms and factories that lie between the mountains and the coast. But what comes out of the tap is used at the expense of the estuary. Before plumbing stretched across the state, that water belonged to the fish.*

Keywords: Chemistry, Infrastructure, Water

---

* The website of the San Francisco Public Utility District reports that the Hetch Hetchy reservoir and aqueduct supply water to approximately 85 percent of the agency's 2,700,000 residential, commercial, and industrial customers in San Francisco, Alameda, San Mateo, and Santa Clara counties.

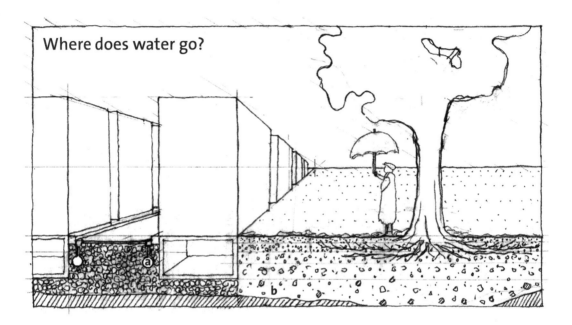

Where does water go?

a. pipe: a cylindrical conduit that carries rain from the surface of the street into the sewer system.

b. percolation: the seeping of water through soil.

13 Pipes

Water moves constantly through land.

Beneath buildings and streets it travels through the sequestered space of the sewer system. Rain that falls on roofs and roadways runs in sheets into gutters. The gutters slope to drains, and the drains connect the surface of the city to pipes underground. Small pipes connect to bigger pipes as more and more drains tie in. Branch lines meet the trunk sewer, and the sewer runs to the bay. Like a freeway, the route is designed for speed: it carries water away as fast as possible.

Below unpaved places, water moves more slowly. Rain drips through the leaves of plants onto the ground and sinks in. Soil is porous, and water percolates through the tiny gaps between its grains. Where the ground is sandy, water moves quickly; where the ground is full of clay, it collects. Sometimes water travels down and sideways to a river or to the sea. Sometimes it emerges from a hillside as a spring. Sometimes it is taken up by the roots of trees, and as the trees transpire, their leaves send it back to the sky.

Keywords: Construction, Souvenir, Water

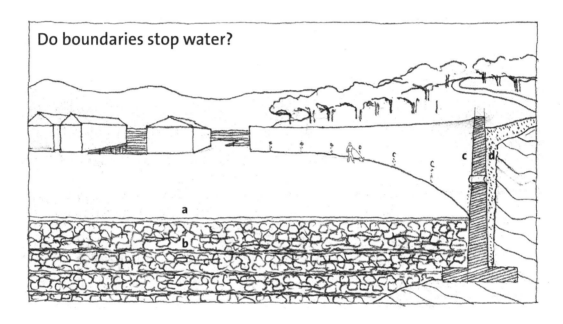

Do boundaries stop water?

a. pavement: a smooth, hard surface designed to bear traffic.
b. water table: the level below which ground is always saturated. In filled land, the water table is at the elevation of the bay.
c. retaining wall: a wall designed to hold back earth.
d. seepage: water that migrates through the tiny spaces in soil.

14 Fort Mason

The US Army needed Fort Mason for two reasons: to keep an eye on the bay, and to gain access to the water. Its lookout occupied the top of Black Point, one of the bedrock hills of the Coast Range. Its supply depot and embarkation point were built on rubble and rocks placed in a marshy cove. Making that significant stretch of filled land demanded the construction of two boundaries: the retaining wall that held back the slope of Black Point, and the pavement that sealed the surface of the new ground.

Both of these boundaries have the same purpose – to control the shape of land – but their structures demand different relationships to the water that moves constantly through this landscape. The wall at Black Point must be perforated by weepholes that allow water to escape from the hill: moisture trapped behind retaining walls undermines their foundations. The pavement beside the wall is impermeable: if the water that washes across it were added to the high water table in the filled land, the ground would be eroded. Rain runs across the surface toward the open water of the bay.

Keywords: Construction, Defense, Land

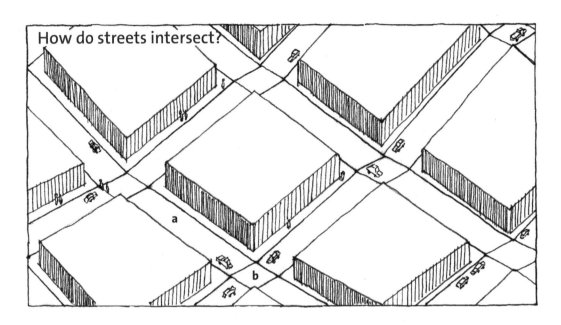

How do streets intersect?

a. street: a public right of way that carries traffic across the city.
b. intersection: the crossing of two streets.

15 Intersections

San Francisco's streets all look the same in the two dimensions of a map, but they vary wildly as they climb relentlessly up and down the city's hills. The result of a national commitment to geometry that made all land equal (at least on paper), the purposeful mismatch between San Francisco's grid and its terrain has produced legendary fingerprints. Some streets turn into stairways, others are divided lengthwise into high and low sides, and many are steep enough to induce vertigo. Views seen from peaks are suddenly lost in valleys and then, like jump cuts at the movies, reappear at closer range on the next ascent. Every trip across town affords a spectacular montage.

These thrills are distractions from a quiet but essential work of urban land art: whatever the pitch of the roadways, their intersections are level. Horizontal punctuation marks in the city's warped grid, street crossings are neutral ground for the negotiation of difference. Their evenness allows otherwise irreconcilable slopes to come together, and in a city where limited visibility demands four-way stop signs, they are places where people almost always wait their turn.

Keywords: Construction

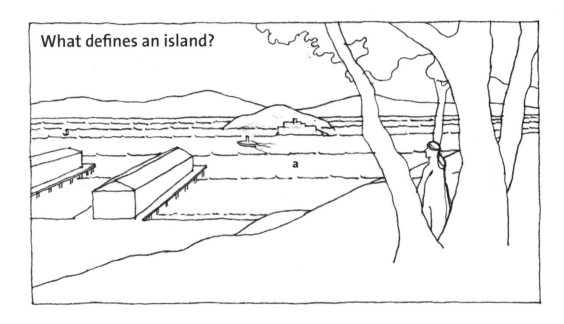

What defines an island?

a.   water: the clear liquid that constitutes seas, bays, lakes, and rivers.

16 Islands

- - - - - - - - - - - - -

Islands are isolated.

Isolation is always defined in opposition to belonging. Geologically, the rocky islands in the bay are part of the Coast Range, the chain of low mountains that extends north from Black Point into Marin and Sonoma Counties, south along the San Francisco Peninsula, and east through Berkeley and Oakland. Ten thousand years ago, the floor of San Francisco Bay was dry, and what we now know as islands were hills. Then the last Ice Age ended. Glaciers melted and the sea level rose. The bay filled up like a bathtub and separated one high point from another. Today the islands are a paradox, in close view of the city but made distant by water. Even their namesakes are elusive – angels for Angel Island and pelicans for Alcatraz.*

Nature has affected culture here: places defined *by* separation have become places defined *for* separation. Federal criminals were incarcerated at Alcatraz. Immigrants from the Pacific Rim were detained at Angel Island, and during the Second World War, German and Japanese prisoners of war were confined there. To be held on the islands was to be isolated: prisoners were cast out of society, and immigrants were kept out. Both islands were legendary. Alcatraz gained fame as an inescapable prison, and Angel Island was the west coast's threshold to a new life in the United States. Now they are tourist attractions, and a trip to the islands is a smaller adventure than before. A journey into exile has become a pleasure cruise.

Islands (and their meanings) are contingent: they come and go with changing circumstances.

Keywords: Water

---

* "Alcatraz" is an archaic Spanish word for pelican. For the history of the islands' names, see Bright, *1500 California Place Names*, 13, 16.

Where is the bay a park?

a. bathhouse: a building where swimmers change clothes; a threshold between land and water.

b. jetty: a small pier; a breakwater constructed to calm waves approaching the shore.

c. cove: a small, sheltered bay.

17 Aquatic Park

At Aquatic Park people play on both sides of the shoreline. The park's New Deal designers reimagined the working waterfront in the service of fun. Instead of the sheds and warehouses where longshoremen moved goods from water to land, architects and artists built a bathhouse where swimmers could change from city clothes into bathing suits. They extended the seawall and disguised it as steps and a beach. They combined a pier and a breakwater in a curving jetty that offered a walk out of town and a long view back. The harbor became a haven, a cove for swimmers and small boats (no motors allowed). The edge of the bay was transformed into a public room.

Seventy-five years later, sunbathers still lounge on the waterfront steps and strollers make their way to the end of the jetty. The bathhouse, no longer their threshold between land and water, has had a checkered history. Closed because of gambling on the premises and then appropriated by the army, it now serves as the home of the Maritime Museum's model ship collection. Grounded on pedestals, the vessels are at least metaphorically at sea. The walls of the pavilion are covered with imaginary underwater creatures, a fantastic vision of aquatic life painted when the building was constructed. And as if to assert its former life, the bathhouse reverberates with the sound of water. It translates the waves that break at its back door into echoes of the bay.*

Keywords: Biology, Interval, Physics, Play

---

* The drawing is based partly on field research and partly on historic images. "Aquatic Park Bathhouse (Maritime Museum): Ayer Murals – San Francisco ca" appears on the website *The Living New Deal*, and the Historic American Buildings Survey's "Aquatic Park Bathhouse (Maritime Museum)," HABS No. ca-2225, appears on the website of the Library of Congress.

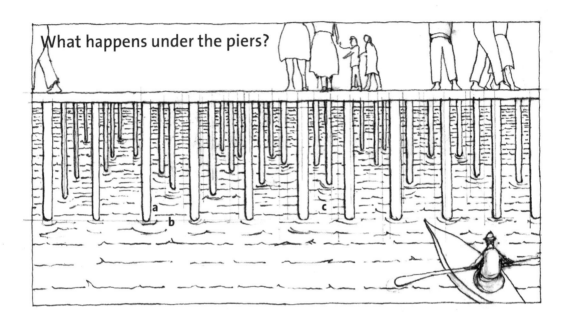

What happens under the piers?

a. piling: a wood or concrete post driven into the floor of the bay to support the horizontal surface of a pier.
b. interference: the change in pattern that occurs when a wave strikes a post or other fixed object.
c. habitat: an environment – natural or constructed – where plants and animals live.

18 Piers

The piers along San Francisco's shore define two landscapes. At the level of the city, piers extend the useful surface of the ground. Built to serve the working harbor, they stretch over the bay so that boats can be loaded and unloaded easily. Their inhabitants come and go between land and water: longshoremen, riggers, sailors, pilots, passengers, tourists, and wanderers.

At the level of the water, the world looks different. The piers act as the ceiling for a dark, quiet space. Light and shadow make moving patterns. The pilings seem to realign themselves as a person moves past, and the waves change shape as they strike the poles. The population beneath the piers is as varied as the crowd above it. Barnacles, worms, skeleton shrimp, sea squirts, and starfish live among the pilings, sometimes alone and sometimes in dense colonies. The piers were built to support culture and commerce, but they provide an unplanned armature for underwater wildlife.

Keywords: Biology, Commerce, Interval, Physics

Who comes together at Fisherman's Wharf?

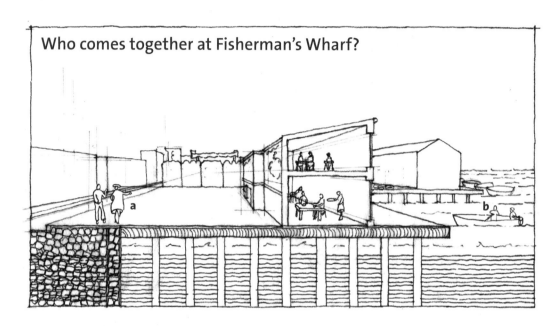

a. diners: people who are eager to eat.
b. fishermen: people who make their living from catching and selling fish.

19 Fisherman's Wharf

Worlds collide at the restaurants on Fisherman's Wharf.

Land meets water and production meets consumption: fishermen dock their boats on the bay side of the wharf to unload their catch, and tourists walk down from the hills to dine on fresh Dungeness crab and cioppino. Fisherman's Wharf also represents a conjunction in time. It is the only place where what remains of San Francisco's working waterfront comes into contact with the city's new tourist economy. Labor meets leisure, but invisibly. The boundary wall of the restaurant hides the working world of the bay from the pleasures of the city. Behind it lie crab pots, nets, boats, and a seamen's chapel. Fish meet the market: wildlife becomes a commodity.

Keywords: Commerce, Play, Work

How does fresh water meet salt water?

a.   salt water: water that carries dissolved salts. Salinity is the measure of saltiness.
b.   fresh water: water that does not carry significant quantities of dissolved salts. The rain, snow, and groundwater that feed lakes and rivers are fresh.
c.   estuary: a zone where the fresh water of a river or stream meets and mixes with the salt water of the ocean. The exchange between salt and fresh water changes with tides and seasons, and its variation creates rich habitat.

20 Salinity

San Francisco Bay is a mixing chamber, the mouth of a great estuary that begins ninety miles east in the California Delta.

Most of the water in the bay comes from the ocean, but not all of it. Fresh water from the western slope of the Sierra Nevada flows through the rivers of the Great Central Valley, across the delta, and past the Carquinez Strait. It emerges into San Pablo Bay as an opposite force to the salt water pushing through the Golden Gate. River meets ocean, but their difference in salinity keeps them apart. The fresh water, less dense than salt water, floats above a wedge of the sea, and they only mix along their boundary.

The seawater wedge migrates toward the Golden Gate during the rainy season, when so much fresh water comes down from the mountains that it pushes the salt water back. In the dry season (or when water is collected behind the state's enormous dams), the river meets the ocean with less force, and the wedge moves east. Twice a day – at high tides – the wedge moves inland, and twice a day – at low tides – it retreats. The Pacific exerts its greatest influence along the deep channel that connects the Golden Gate to Carquinez Strait: salt water pulses north and south from that line as the tide ebbs and flows. In the southern part of San Francisco Bay, far from the outlet of the Sierra's great rivers and beyond the main reach of the tides, the relationship between salt and fresh water depends on what flows down from the Coast Range and through nearby towns. Each river, creek, and outlet makes its own estuary, and water mixes at local scales.

Keywords: Biology, Chemistry, Interval, Water

Why do walls crack?

a. retaining wall: a wall designed to hold back earth.

b. crack: a linear fissure in a surface that has split but not yet broken into separate parts.

c. volunteer: a plant that emerges spontaneously where it finds soil and space.

d. weephole: a small hole that allows water to escape from the ground behind a retaining wall.

21 Cracks

Retaining walls maintain controlled elevations.

Those words tell the story of how walls lay claim to land. Retain, from the Latin word *retinere* – to hold back – implies possession: keeping something in place and engaging it in service. Maintain, from *manu tenere* – to hold in the hand – involves constancy: keeping something in good repair and ensuring that it stays in working order.

Walls have turned San Francisco from a cluster of uninhabitable hills into a city's worth of building sites, plus roads and stairs to get from one place to another. These claims do not go uncontested. Nothing stays still in landscapes, and the earth works against every wall that holds it back. Soil shifts and settles all the time. Earthquakes shake the ground in sudden starts. Water seeps and pools behind foundations. Tree roots push against anything in their way. Sooner or later, even the sturdiest wall cracks. One crack leads to another. Crevices and gaps become habitat for plants that grow in stony soil. Left alone, the wall would crumble, and the hill it interrupted would return to its angle of repose.

Keywords: Biology, Defense, Infrastructure, Land, Water

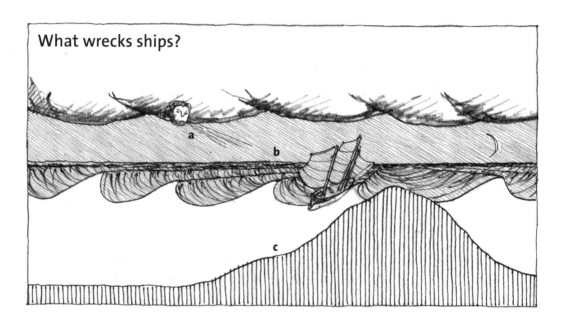

What wrecks ships?

a.   wind: the natural movement of air across water and land.

b.   fog: water vapor condensed in a mass just above the level of the bay.

c.   rock: a knob of hard mineral material that protrudes above or lurks below the surface of the sea.

22 Shipwrecks

Shipwrecks occur with the multiplication of hazards: high winds push boats against rocky shores, for instance, or erratic currents carry them onto shoals and shallows. San Francisco Bay, the Golden Gate, and the near reaches of the Pacific coast present a broad inventory of complementary dangers. Prevailing northwesterly winds blow toward the rocky shoreline. The narrow strait and the sandbar just beyond it create fast, unpredictable currents and strong eddies. Fog limits visibility. Drifting sediment changes the depth of the bay floor. A chain of rocks, reduced by dynamite but still present underwater, makes a treacherous diagonal line from just off the coast at North Point to the Golden Gate.

San Francisco Bay was the main port on the west coast in the century after the Gold Rush; it saw thousands of vessels come and go. The higher the volume of traffic, the greater the chance of a wreck. Ships of all kinds – traders, whalers, passenger ships, fishing boats, lumber boats, tugs, tankers, cargo ships, and naval vessels – were wholly or partly lost to bad weather and unseen dangers. From time to time, old shipwrecks come to light, exposed by the scouring of heavy storms. Their remains are excavated, cataloged, and held in the public trust as material records of the bay's cultural history.

Keywords: Souvenir

How does water change light?

a. interface: a surface that makes a boundary between two substances. Light is transformed when it meets the interface between air and water.

b. interruption: a figure or object that prevents the sun's light from reaching the surface of the water.

c. shadow: the absence of light registered on an opaque surface. When water is cloudy, its interface with air changes, and light makes shadows instead of reflections.

23 Light

Light traveling from the transparent medium of air into the transparent medium of water is partly reflected and partly refracted. Reflected light is bent back at the water's surface. The water acts like a mirror. It makes an image of what's beside or above it: the sky, the lights on the Bay Bridge, the boats in the harbor. Refracted light enters the water, but it bends as it crosses the surface. The water acts like a lens. It distorts the images of objects that are partly submerged: the piers along the waterfront, the hulls of boats, the fish that come to the surface.

The water in the bay changes from place to place and from moment to moment, so its effects on light vary. Waves break up reflections. Depth affects color, and so does the concentration of minerals and microscopic plants and animals. We think of water as clear, but sometimes it's cloudy. Washed down from the mountains or floating up from the bay floor, tiny bits of dissolved land interfere with its transparency and change its optical behavior. Its surface makes a projection screen, and the water registers unexpected shadows.

Water shows us images of the world – and sometimes, of ourselves. If Narcissus had stood beside the bay, its cloudiness might have saved him from his vanity. Caught between the water and the afternoon sun, his beauty would have been hidden in a silhouette.

Keywords: Physics, Play

What gave Telegraph Hill value?

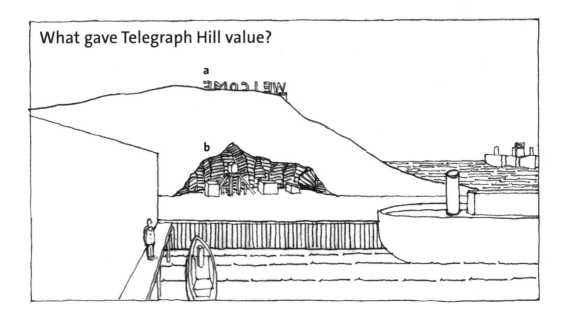

a.   signal: a gesture, sign, shape, or sound that conveys information.

b.   quarry: an excavation blasted and cut to provide stone and rock for building.

24 Telegraph Hill

From San Francisco's earliest days, Telegraph Hill was valuable for its image and its substance.

The hill's unmistakable appearance made it a landmark on the US Navy's early charts of San Francisco Bay. Because it could be seen from the bay, the harbor, and the city, a semaphore telegraph station operated there during the early 1850s. For nearly fifty years, a time ball at the summit allowed ship captains to calibrate their chronometers. In 1908, San Francisco's first greeting to Roosevelt's Great White Fleet was a sign at the top of Greenwich Street. Big enough to be recognized from thirty miles away, it read, "WELCOME."

At the same moment that Telegraph Hill's visual presence made it important to sailors and surveyors, its slopes were being chipped away to provide ballast for vessels leaving San Francisco without cargo. Starting in the late 1860s, its eastern side was quarried for stone to build the seawall and pave the city's streets. Excavation continued until 1914, half a dozen years after Roosevelt's ships sailed past the welcome sign. By then, the hill's face was a cliff – steep, fractured, and unstable.

Telegraph Hill is a paradox. It has offered San Francisco advantages in its persistence and in its removal.

Keywords: Land, Navigation, Souvenir

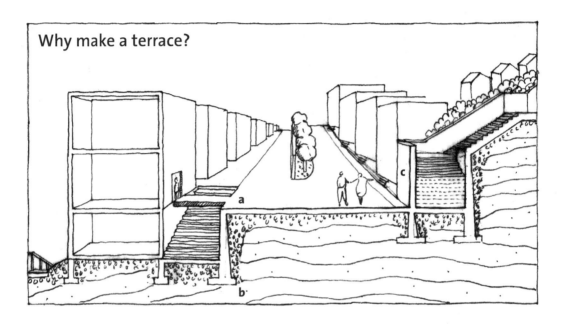

Why make a terrace?

a. terrace: ground made level (or less steep) by carving away or filling in a hill.

b. retaining wall: a wall designed to hold back earth.

c. cheek wall: a wall that forms the edge of a stair.

25 Terrace

Built to make useful ground from slopes that are too steep to inhabit, terraces are uphill
cousins to the filled land at the water's edge. They rely on the interruption of a slope by a
retaining wall. Land on either side of the wall is excavated or filled to make level surfaces,
and the incline is transformed into two spaces separated by a vertical drop.

The terraces that surround the intersection of Greenwich and Montgomery Streets
allow the everyday spaces of the city to occupy a difficult site. They make building lots:
stepped one by one, each house has a front door at its own elevation. They create streets
level enough for cars to manage: Montgomery's east side and north end are held up by
retaining walls, and from Union Street to Greenwich Street, another wall along its center-
line splits it into high and low lanes. They allow pedestrians to climb the hill: the flights
of the Greenwich Street stairs are strings of terraces scaled for walking. The intersection
is a concentrated expression of accommodations that occur all over San Francisco. A city
built on hills is inevitably a city of terraces: retaining walls change even precipitous slopes
into real estate.

Keywords: Construction, Infrastructure

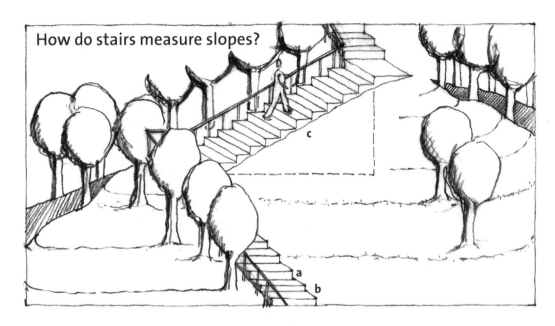

How do stairs measure slopes?

a. riser: the vertical face of a stair.
b. tread: the horizontal surface of a stair.
c. slope: the hypotenuse of the right triangle formed by all the risers and treads of a stairway.

26 Stairs

The stairways on Telegraph Hill transform a steep slope into brief intervals of level ground. With its horizontal treads and vertical risers, each flight of steps comprises a string of small terraces. Stairs project an angled line – the pitch of the hill – into a series of right triangles. The dimensions of the triangles come from the dimensions of human bodies. They are designed for walking, and the climb from Sansome Street to Coit Tower translates the hill into physical experience.

Between Montgomery Street and the top of the hill, the Filbert and Greenwich stairs run straight up the slope. The Filbert stair extends the city's asphalt grid as a wooden construction. It sits above the ground, and its shadow reveals the incline of its hypotenuse. The Greenwich stair, built of brick and concrete, is set into the ground. It traces the hill's angle with its retaining walls and handrails. Below Montgomery, the stairs cover such precipitous terrain that a route perpendicular to the slope would be too steep to negotiate gracefully. To make a shallower course, the stairs run at a diagonal to the slope. Like a switchback path in the mountains, they turn to lengthen the distance along which they descend.

San Francisco's hills form its harbor – and its image – but they are not easy to occupy. Stairs are like piers: they extend the inhabitable surface of the ground.

Keywords: Construction, Play

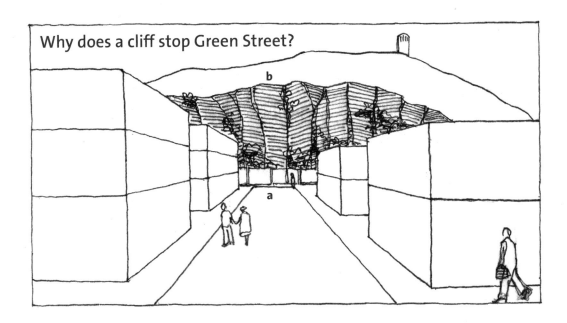

Why does a cliff stop Green Street?

a.   street: a public right of way that carries traffic across the city. San Francisco's streets run in straight lines without reference to topography.

b.   cliff: a high, nearly vertical rock face.

27 Cliff

The eastern stretch of Green Street starts at the water's edge and crosses land made by piling rubble on a tidal marsh. It stops just west of Sansome Street, brought to a dead halt by the cliff at Telegraph Hill. In its beginning is its end: the seawall at the Embarcadero was made of rock blasted from the hill.

Quarried for nearly half a century, the eastern slope of Telegraph Hill was used to build the city. Green Street ends at the largest excavation, the Gray Brothers Quarry.* Cutting away solid ground to fill the shore was less straightforward than it seemed. The new stability at the water's edge was achieved by undermining the hill. Blasting caused landslides; deep cracks destroyed the integrity of the rock; and houses above the excavations collapsed spontaneously. One hundred years after the quarries closed, the east face of Telegraph Hill is held in place by nets and retaining walls. These tenuous means to keep the cliff from tumbling onto Sansome Street bear witness to the complexities of addition and subtraction.

Keywords: Land, Souvenir

---

* The chapters "Early Quarries and the Sea Wall" and "The Gray Brothers, Incredible Quarrymen" in David Myrick's *San Francisco's Telegraph Hill* provide a detailed history of the twin processes of quarrying and landmaking and of the consequent destabilization of Telegraph Hill's eastern face. The Gray brothers, who operated their quarry from the 1890s until 1914, were the most aggressive and venal of the hill's exploiters.

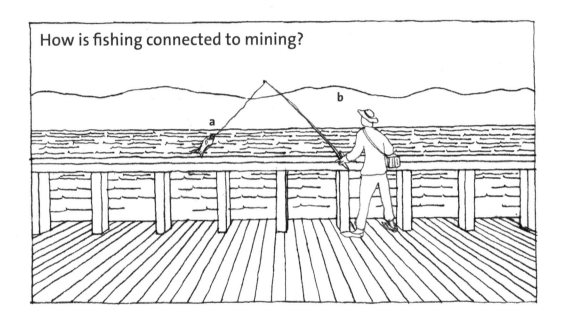

How is fishing connected to mining?

a. fish: vertebrates that live in water and breathe through gills. San Francisco Bay supports a great range of fish species, substantial commercial fisheries, and countless sport fishermen.

b. watershed: a region bounded by a ridgeline. All of the water within a watershed's boundaries flows to the same end point. San Francisco Bay belongs to the vast watersheds of the Sacramento and San Joaquin Rivers, which flow from the Sierra Nevada, and it belongs to the small watersheds that drain the hills of the Bay Area.

28 Fishing

A fisherman on Pier 7 might not know that the fish on his line ties him to the Gold Rush. The story begins in 1845, when Mexican colonists realized that the cinnabar at New Almaden was raw material for mercury. They began refining it just in time to send vast quantities to the mines of the Sierra Nevada, where it was used to separate gold and silver from ore and sediment. Carried by the detritus of hydraulic mining, millions of pounds of mercury traveled through the rivers of central California and ended up on the floor of northern San Francisco Bay. The New Almaden cinnabar mine was a culprit, too: its abandoned remnants still send mercury through local streams to the bay's southern reaches.

We say that changeable people are mercurial because elemental mercury can be so radically transformed. The mercury in the bay began as cinnabar rocks. Crushed and heated, the rocks produced vapor; collected and cooled, the vapor condensed into mercury. Sent to the Sierras, the mercury bonded with tiny particles of gold and silver and made them heavy enough to harvest. Carried by rivers to the bay, mercury that was metabolized by aquatic bacteria became methyl mercury, a poison that acts on the nervous system. The methyl mercury traveled – and still travels – through the food chain. It contaminates plankton when it is excreted by bacteria; it contaminates small fish that eat bacteria and plankton; it contaminates big fish that eat small fish; and it contaminates people who eat big fish. At each step, the poison becomes more concentrated.

Fishing in the bay means fishing in a watershed where the past is not a foreign country.

Keywords: Commerce, Souvenir, Water

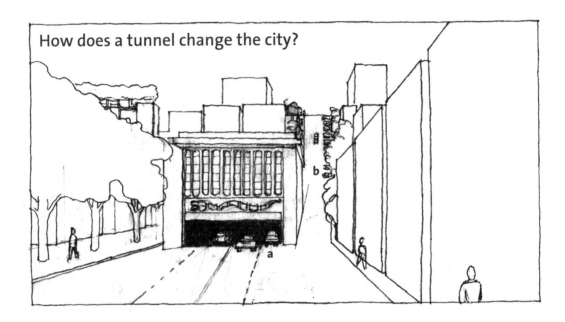

How does a tunnel change the city?

a. shortcut: an alternative route that is quicker, simpler, or easier than the usual way of getting somewhere.

b. slope: the inclined surface of a hill; the vertical change covered over a horizontal distance. In the two blocks between Mason Street and its crest at Jones Street, Broadway rises nearly 150 feet.

29 Tunnel

- - - - - - - - - - - - -

San Francisco's steep hills divide the city. Obstacles to traffic, they limit speeds and wear out brakes and clutches.

Until the construction of the Broadway Tunnel, Russian Hill separated the waterfront from points west. Finished in 1952, the tunnel makes a level line under the precipitous slopes that climb and descend the crest of the hill. A fast route across town, it runs straight from Mason Street to Larkin and connects the mansions of Cow Hollow and Pacific Heights to the towers of the Financial District.

The tunnel belongs to a series of constructions that make hilly terrain less inconvenient. Like the Bay Bridge, it was built as a topographic shortcut. Its means are different – a bore rather than a series of spans – but its goal is the same: to speed travel around the city. Proposed in a 1948 transportation plan* to link the Embarcadero and Central Freeways, the Broadway Tunnel is a not-so-distant cousin of the city's constructed waterfront. Just as the piers remade the shore for the convenience of boats, the tunnel reconfigured Russian Hill for California's new favorite vehicles: cars.

Keywords: Interval

---

* The plan for the Broadway Tunnel and its associated freeways was described in the San Francisco Department of City Planning, *Progress in City Planning*, 10–13, and pictured in the drawing "(San Francisco) Comprehensive trafficways plan: Trafficways 11 Plate 8," which appears on the website of the David Rumsey Historical Map Collection.

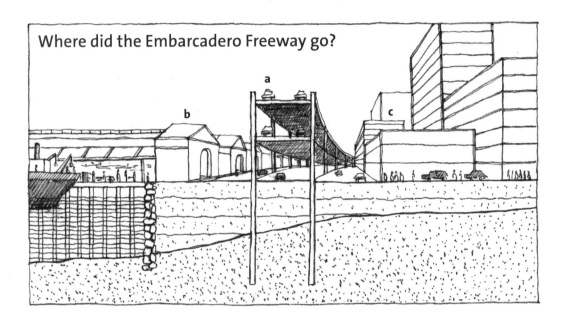

Where did the Embarcadero Freeway go?

a. freeway: a road whose limited connection to its surroundings allows travel at high speeds.
b. port: a stretch of waterfront where wharves and piers enable the landing and loading of ships.
c. city: a place where people, capital, institutions, and culture are concentrated.

30 Embarcadero

San Francisco was born a port city. Goods and dollars flowed back and forth from water to land. Seamen lifted cargo into and out of ships; stevedores and longshoremen moved it along wharves; teamsters hauled it to and from warehouses; clerks kept track of what came and went; brokers matched freight to ships; merchants and traders bought and sold raw materials and finished goods; bankers held profits and covered losses. For San Francisco's first half-century, there was no way to draw a line between the port and the city. When the seawall and piers were redesigned in the late nineteenth and early twentieth centuries, their construction included a continuous working boulevard along the wharves and warehouses. In 1909 it was named the Embarcadero: the landing place.

Fifty years later, the Embarcadero Freeway was built above and beside the roadway to serve a different set of connections. A fast route to the Bay Bridge and the new freeways to the south, it tied old San Francisco to new suburbs. Loud, tough, and two stories high, it stood between the port and the city for more than thirty years. Damaged beyond repair by the Loma Prieta earthquake, the freeway was demolished in 1991. When its disappearance brought the shoreline back into view, the port was quiet. The wharves were still there, but ship traffic had moved to Oakland. Bankers and merchants who crossed the Embarcadero found birdwatchers and sightseers instead of seamen and stevedores.

Keywords: Commerce, Infrastructure, Intervals, Souvenir, Work

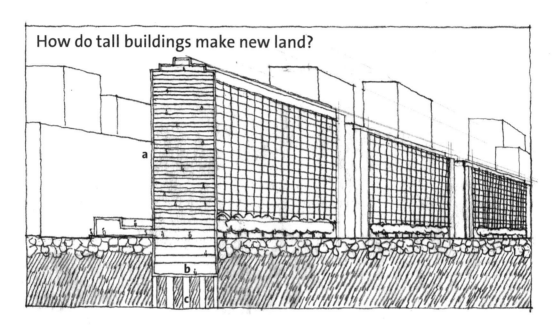

How do tall buildings make new land?

a. vertical land: new surfaces constructed as the multiple floors of high-rise structures.

b. underground land: new surfaces excavated from fill and contained in the bases of towers.

c. foundation: the lowest part of a tall building, constructed to transfer its weight from the ground's unstable surface to the solid rock that lies below soil, fill, gravel, and mud.

31 Tall Buildings

Once, new land at the edge of the bay was built horizontally. Piers extended streets into the mudflats of Yerba Buena Cove. Rubble and sand were placed beside and between the piers to raise the surface of the flats. The seawall was constructed to stop the filled ground from eroding. Land was made for access to the water because the city lived on maritime commerce.

Today, new land is made vertically. The stacked floors of the Embarcadero Center multiplied the surface of the ground dozens of times, and its garages made inhabitable space underground. Built between 1967 and 1981, as ship traffic was moving from San Francisco to Oakland, the center's towers defined a new world on the waterfront. Office workers replaced longshoremen, and access to the bay was less important than easy connections to subways and freeways. Sometimes cities are made gradually, but the Embarcadero Center was part of a rapid process of urban renewal fueled by suspicion of the old, enabled by public policy that swept away anything decrepit, and bankrolled by real estate speculation. The compound and its neighbors, high-rise buildings linked by walkways two stories above the street, crowded out the warehouses of the Produce District.

In this vertical city, the filled land at the shore is uncertain ground. It does not have the structural strength to support tall buildings, and earthquakes have the power to shake it into a liquid. The Embarcadero Center's towers extend far below the surface of the waterfront. Their foundations reach through sixteen stories' worth of rubble and mud to bedrock, and their bases are designed as giant shock absorbers.

Keywords: Commerce, Construction, Land, Work

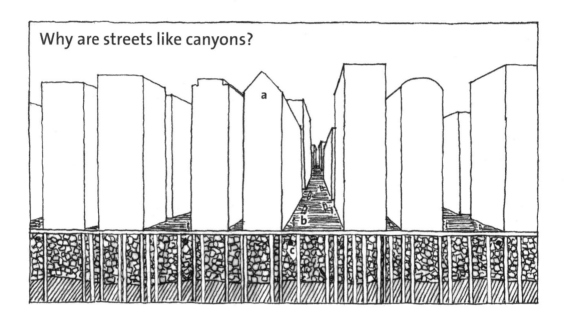

Why are streets like canyons?

a. skyscraper: a building so tall that it blocks the view of the sky from the street.

b. street: a public thoroughfare that crosses the city at ground level.

c. pier: a vertical support that transfers the weight of a tall building from the ground's unstable surface to the solid rock that lies below soil, fill, gravel, and mud.

32 Canyons

Seen from across the bay, the jagged skyline of San Francisco's Financial District looks like a mountain range. On the ground, the streets feel like canyons – deep, dark, chilly.

The relationships are not only metaphorical. The wealth that built office towers on the filled land at Yerba Buena Cove emerged from the Sierra Nevada. In 1847, San Francisco was a town of fewer than five hundred people. The Gold Rush turned it into an instant city, a major port, a depot for goods, a hub for immigration, a manufacturing center, and a parking place for cash. San Francisco became the financial capital of the west coast, but at a price: the hydraulic mining that funded growth washed away vast stretches of the Sierra. A century and a half later, the glass and steel monuments along Montgomery and Market Streets still reflect the gold and silver torn from the mountains.

Keywords: Commerce, Souvenir

Where are ships buried?

a. ship: a vessel that navigates deep waters and long distances.

b. piling: a heavy post driven into the ground at the water's edge to support a pier.

c. archaeologist: a scholar who studies a past culture by excavating and analyzing its material artifacts.

33 Buried Ships

The land between the Bay Bridge and the Exploratorium is a graveyard for ships: traces of San Francisco's first port lie buried there.

In the year between December 1848 and December 1849, more than 750 vessels sailed for San Francisco from American ports. They landed at Yerba Buena Cove, at the base of San Francisco's eastern hills. A mud flat when the tide was out and shallow water when it came in, the cove was transformed by the instant city that sprang up with the Gold Rush. Businessmen and speculators dumped sand and garbage to fill in the water's edge. They threw up buildings on piles and extended long piers across the flats to reach deep anchorages. Just offshore, the cove was filled with ships. Some came and went. Others stayed to serve as *ad hoc* warehouses and offices, floating beside the piers or dragged up onto the mud.*

In 1851, a fire destroyed much of San Francisco and its harbor. Nine square blocks of piers, buildings, and ships burned and collapsed into Yerba Buena Cove. The area was quickly filled in with sand, and the ruins were preserved under mud and water. No one knows exactly how many boats are hidden below the waterfront. Abandoned by their crews, broken up for parts, and covered as the city's shoreline was built out, they number in the dozens. From time to time they come to light, revealed by the excavation of foundations for new construction.

Keywords: Commerce, Work

---

* Maritime archaeologist James Delgado's book *Gold Rush Port*, 51–90, gives a vivid account of the establishment, destruction, burial, and excavation of the waterfront community at Yerba Buena Cove. The drawing for this field entry is based on his photograph "The hull of the *General Harrison* buried in the heart of San Francisco," 24.

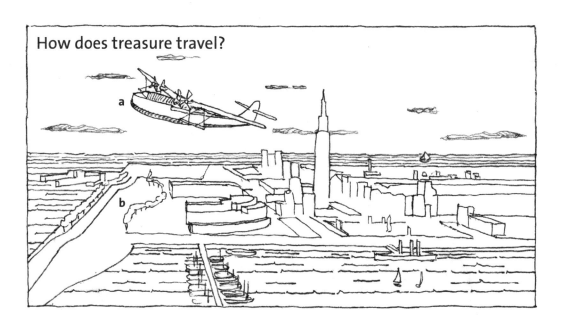

How does treasure travel?

a. flying boat: a plane that landed on open water. Before the widespread construction of long runways, flying boats could be made bigger than planes that landed on the ground.
b. Treasure Island: an island built on top of Yerba Buena Shoals to provide land for the 1939 World's Fair and the San Francisco terminal of Pan American World Airways.

34 Treasure

The first commercial flight across the Pacific Ocean carried a treasure of the time: 110,000 pieces of mail.

In 1935, Pan American Airways inaugurated its trans-Pacific service with a Martin M-130 flying boat, the *China Clipper*. Named for the fast nineteenth-century sailing ships that carried small, precious cargoes – opium, tea, and silk – from London to the Far East, the *Clipper* flew from San Francisco Bay to Manila by way of Honolulu, Midway Island, Wake Island, and Guam. The flight time was just under sixty hours; six days in total, the journey was more than two weeks faster than a regularly scheduled steamship crossing. Passenger service to Hong Kong and Manila began the following year on Pan Am's expanded clipper fleet. In 1939, after Treasure Island was built, the flying boats came and went from the cove to its south, their takeoffs and landings an additional spectacle for the World's Fair. The story changed when the Second World War broke out. The navy commandeered Pan Am's clippers and transformed Treasure Island into an airbase. The Martin flying boats were lost in combat, and no more were built. Like their namesakes, they had been made obsolete by new infrastructure. Just as the Suez Canal gave steamships the advantage over sailing ships, runways built for the military supported civilian traffic in airplanes that landed on the ground.

Today airmail is ordinary, but time is still money. Now treasure travels from San Francisco to Manila as fast as a courier can carry it: by jet, overnight.*

Keywords: Interval, Navigation, Play

----

* This drawing is based on two photographs: one of the fair, "Aerial View," on the University of Maryland's website *A Treasury of World's Fair Art & Architecture*, and "The *China Clipper* passes over the San Francisco waterfront," on the website *The Flying Clippers*.

Are islands and shoals the same?

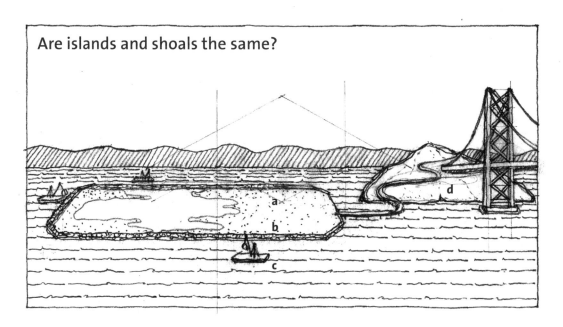

a. shoal: a place where the bay floor is close to the surface of the water.
b. seawall: a wall built to contain filled land and protect it from erosion.
c. dredge: a boat equipped with machinery to lift and transport sediment from the bay floor.
d. bedrock: solid rock that lies below the surface of the ground. The bedrock of the Coast Range was pushed into low mountains by the movement of tectonic plates that underlie the Pacific Ocean and North America.

35 Shoals

- - - - - - - - - - - - -

Yerba Buena Island and Treasure Island make a pair, but they are not twins.

Yerba Buena belongs to the geological formation of the Coast Range, a consequence of the movement of tectonic plates that make up the Earth's outer layer. Between three and four million years ago, the plate under the Pacific Ocean began to slide northward against the edge of the plate that supports North America. Folded and crumpled by the friction, the North American seafloor was pushed up into a line of low mountains on the edge of the continent. Ten thousand years ago, when the last Ice Age ended, Yerba Buena was separated from its neighbors by rising water in San Francisco Bay. The mountain became an island.

Treasure Island is a younger construction, the product of dredges and siphons. Until the 1930s it was Yerba Buena Shoals, a high patch of bay floor just north of Yerba Buena Island. It presented a significant navigation hazard – some parts lay just a few feet below the water – and in 1936, the federal government's Works Progress Administration undertook its transformation into useful ground. Sand and sediment dredged from around the bay were piled behind a seawall built of rubble blasted from the Yerba Buena Tunnel. The new land was dedicated almost exactly a year after the Bay Bridge connected San Francisco to Oakland. Treasure Island is a closer relative of the bridge than of the old island: both projects were undertaken to expand the territory of a watery metropolis.*

Keywords: Defense, Land, Water

---

* The depiction of Treasure Island's construction is based on a 1937 photograph by the War Department, Office of the Chief of Engineers, San Francisco District, "(032-32E-88)(4-2-37-9:35A)(12-12000) Yerba Buena Shoal Fill," on the website of the National Archives and Records Administration.

What supports the bridge?

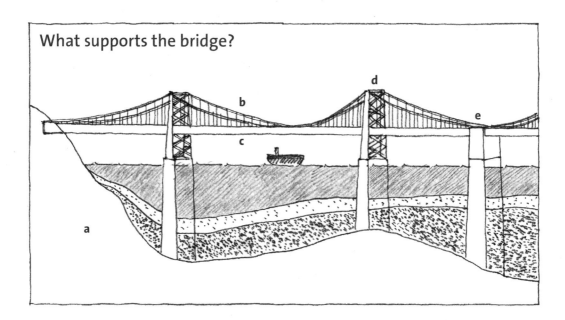

a. bedrock: the solid rock that lies under soil and sediment.
b. cable: a bundle of steel strands compressed in a steel casing.
c. deck: the travel surface of a bridge.
d. tower: the tall, slender structure that carries the cables of a suspension bridge.
e. anchorage: the structure to which suspension cables are fixed.

36 Bridge

The deck of the Bay Bridge is a strip of continuous ground between San Francisco and Oakland. It flouts the limits of landmass, but it rests on bedrock.

The bridge's iconic western half is made of two suspension spans, one a mirror of the other. Each begins from an anchorage point in solid rock – one embedded in Yerba Buena Island and the other in Rincon Hill – and they meet at a constructed island halfway in between: the Center Anchorage, which contains more concrete than the Empire State Building. The cables that hold the bridge deck are suspended from two concrete and steel towers and pulled tight at each anchorage. The tension in the cables transfers the weight of the deck to the towers and anchorages, which send it to the bedrock below.

The bridges' ability to transfer weight vertically allows them to carry cars horizontally: 270,000 vehicles a day roll across their constructed surface.*

Keywords: Infrastructure, Interval, Navigation, Souvenir

---

* This drawing is based on an illustration in E. Cromwell Mensch's *San Francisco Oakland Bay Bridge*, 4.

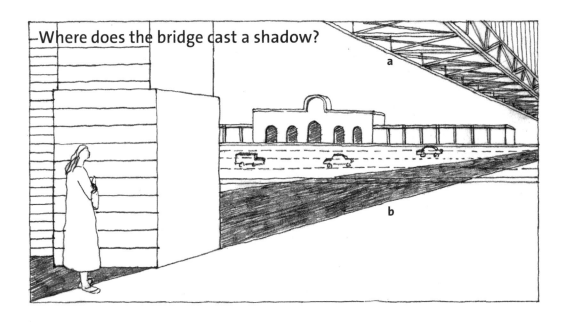

Where does the bridge cast a shadow?

a. span: a segment of a bridge; the distance over which a bridge or bridge segment extends.

b. shadow: the absence of light registered on an opaque surface.

37 Shadow

The Bay Bridge casts a shadow on the Embarcadero.

The change in light points to a long-forgotten disappearance. The shadow falls on what used to be a marshy shore: the Embarcadero runs across land constructed to support the growth of the city. Territorial expansion does not mean the extension of bearing capacity, though. The bridge's westernmost cables must tie back to the bedrock of Rincon Hill, blocks past the constructed shoreline. The last spans of the bridge hover above the soft ground between the seawall and the *terra firma* of old land. The shadow on the Embarcadero is a geological clue hidden in plain sight.

In some ways the Embarcadero and the bridge are opposites. One hides its structure and the other shows it. One is low and the other is high. One was built to serve ships and the other to serve cars. One occupies the bay as a mass and the other traverses it as a span. In other ways, the two constructions are twins, products of the same logic. Both were built as points of embarkation and arrival. Both extended San Francisco's reach. Both denied the bay as a boundary. Both changed the definition of the edge of the city: the Embarcadero moved it east to the seawall, and the Bay Bridge stretched it far beyond the horizon.

Keywords: Souvenir

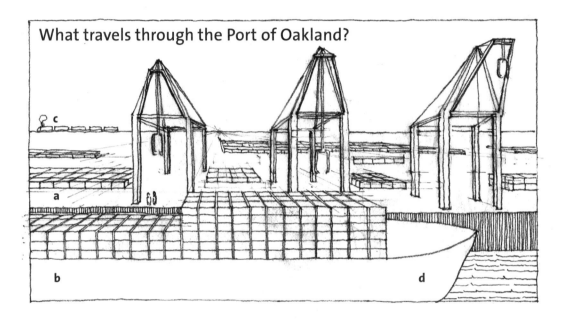

What travels through the Port of Oakland?

a. cargo: goods and commodities carried as freight by ships, trains, and trucks. Break bulk cargo is packed in small units – bales, bags, boxes, or barrels – or as individual items; bulk cargo is transported, unpackaged, in large quantities.
b. ship: a large vessel that navigates deep waters and long distances.
c. train: a series of linked cars pushed or pulled by locomotives along railroads.
d. ballast water: water carried in a ship's hold so that its weight will increase the vessel's stability.

38 Port

The Port of Oakland lies at the center of a map of the world. Shipping routes to and from here go everywhere. Half of the goods that arrive in the United States and a third of what leaves travel through California, and Oakland handles almost all of the shipping in the northern part of the state. Its biggest exports are dried fruit, nuts, and meat. Its biggest imports are machinery and electronics. Some of what comes and goes is unintended: animals and plants traveling from foreign ports in ballast water establish themselves in the bay and wreak havoc on native species.

The port rose to prominence in the 1960s, when it led the use of new shipping practices. Before the Second World War, break bulk cargo was packed in boxes and barrels – or even as individual items – and loaded and unloaded piece by piece by riggers and longshoremen. After the war, Canadians and Americans designed large steel containers that could be loaded at the source, sent overland to port, carried across the ocean, and transferred from ships to trains and trucks without ever being opened: cargo could go straight from senders to recipients. Because the transfers were mechanized, handling times were much faster. The new technology made international trade cheap, and the new math of commerce transformed the harbor. Ships grew too big to berth at finger piers. Huge cargo volumes demanded vast staging areas for sea-to-land transfer. Roads and train tracks had to be rerouted to serve ports efficiently. Oakland's waterfront adapted, but San Francisco's became obsolete. As cranes replaced dockworkers, the region's main port moved to the east side of the bay.

Keywords: Commerce, Infrastructure, Work

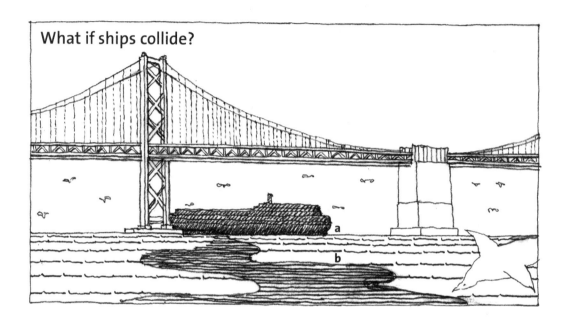

a. tank: a reservoir that holds fuel. Container ships carry fuel for their journeys. Tankers carry fuel as cargo.

b. slick: a thin film of oil that floats on the surface of water. As the oil encounters the shoreline, it covers wetlands, rocks, and beaches. When it comes into contact with birds and animals, it coats their feathers and fur.

39 Collision

Shipping is profitable – and risky. San Francisco Bay is hard to navigate, and the vessels that cross it carry hazardous cargoes and huge quantities of fuel.

Since the passage of the US Environmental Protection Act, the bay has suffered two devastating oil spills, both products of bad judgment under difficult circumstances. In 1971, a tanker leaving Standard Oil's Richmond dock collided with an inbound ship just west of the Golden Gate Bridge. Its fuel tanks were pierced, and as the two vessels drifted across the bay, more than 800,000 gallons of partly refined oil poured onto the surface of the water. The slick spread from Point Reyes to Half Moon Bay. Seven thousand oiled birds were collected. Three hundred survived. Afterward, all ships were required to participate in the Coast Guard's Vessel Traffic Service. Even so, in 2007, a container ship hit a Bay Bridge tower west of Yerba Buena Island. Its hull sustained a gash more than 200 feet long, and currents and tides carried 58,000 gallons of heavy fuel oil north to San Pablo Bay, south beyond Hunters Point, and west past the Golden Gate. Nearly three thousand oiled birds were collected. Only four hundred birds recovered enough to be released. The Pacific herring population was decimated.

When catastrophe occurs, restitution is measured in dollars. Some losses are easy to quantify and to pay back: the cost of repairs to a ship or a bridge tower, or the funds spent to mobilize equipment that contains an oil slick. But what compensates for the death of the birds and the fish?*

Keywords: Interval, Navigation

---

* This drawing is based on Michael Macor's photograph in "Container Ship Hits Bay Bridge Tower – Fuel Spills, but Span Undamaged," *San Francisco Chronicle,* 8 November 2007.

Where do houseboats belong?

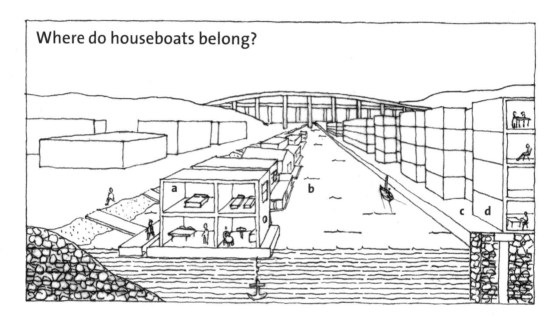

a. houseboat: a boat or barge modified to serve as a dwelling place and permanently anchored alongshore.
b. channel: a navigable waterway left open during the construction of new land. Mission Creek Channel is the last trace of water in Mission Bay.
c. filled land: new ground constructed along the shore by placing rubble and sand in marshes and shallow water.
d. apartment house: a residential building divided into units for people who live separately.

40 Houseboats

Even though they float, the houseboats along Mission Creek Channel are tethered to the systems of the city: streets, sewers, water lines, power grids, and tax rolls.

Like the houseboats, the channel and the neighborhood belong to both the bay and the city. In 1860, South Beach was San Francisco's southern limit. Mission Bay, the mouth of the creek that ran from Mission Dolores to the shore, was a shallow cove between two rocky promontories. As the construction of Long Bridge extended Fourth Street to the base of Potrero Hill, the city moved in. Shipbuilders took over the cove, and factories lined its edges. Even when it was filled, Mission Bay remained tied to the shore. Warehouses replaced shipyards, and commercial boats docked at Mission Creek to load and unload their cargoes. The houseboats arrived in 1960; as shipping declined, they presided over a view of the bay and the sky.

In the last dozen years, San Francisco has reinhabited Mission Bay. Full of big new buildings, the neighborhood looks like *terra firma*. The only trace of water is in the channel where Mission Creek escapes from pipes. The old headlands of Steamboat Point and Potrero Point are embedded in new land. Mission Creek Channel and the houseboats are an exception to the dense fabric of the city, a vestige of its vanished life on the shore.

Keywords: Land, Play

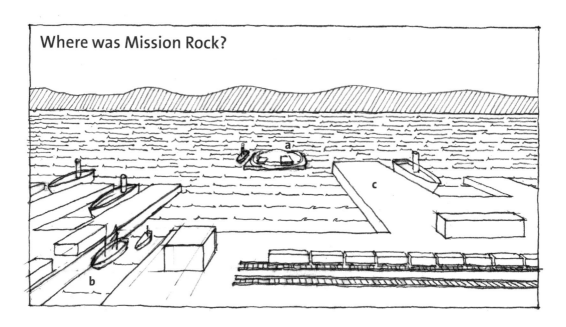

Where was Mission Rock?

a. rock: a knob of hard mineral material that protrudes above the surface of the sea.
b. channel: a navigable waterway left open during the construction of new land. Mission Creek Channel is the last trace of water in Mission Bay.
c. pier: a platform built out from the shore to serve as a mooring place for ships.

41 Mission Rock

Mission Rock appears on the earliest maps of San Francisco, lying off the coast at Mission Bay. Smaller than an island, it was big enough to be useful as an anchoring point; enlarged by ballast rocks, it was put into service as a grain terminal. The shoreline inched closer and closer: Mission Bay was filled, and piers stretched into the bay. In the end, Mission Rock was swallowed whole by San Francisco's expanding port. Shortly after the Second World War, the rock was burned, leveled, and embedded in the new land of Pier 50, also known as Mission Rock Terminal. It persists in two monuments: as a stepping stone in the pavement and at the Mission Rock Resort, a bait shop turned dive bar turned trendy dinner spot.

Before San Francisco drew a firm line between land and water, offshore rocks – like inland marshes – made the shoreline ambiguous. As wetlands were filled to make land more solid, rocks were removed to make water more open. The most spectacular disappearance was the explosion of Blossom Rock, which lay just under the water northeast of North Point. In 1870, nearly fifty years after it was charted as a shipping hazard, it was blasted to bits under the auspices of the Corps of Engineers. Crowds attended the event, and newspapers reported it.* Harding Rock, Arch Rock, and Shag Rocks, Blossom's neighbors in a chain that ended at Alcatraz, fell victim to dynamite as well. Reduced, like Blossom, to depths some forty feet below the bay, their only visible traces are marks on sailors' charts.

Keywords: Interval, Land

---

* See Williamson and Heuer, *Report*.

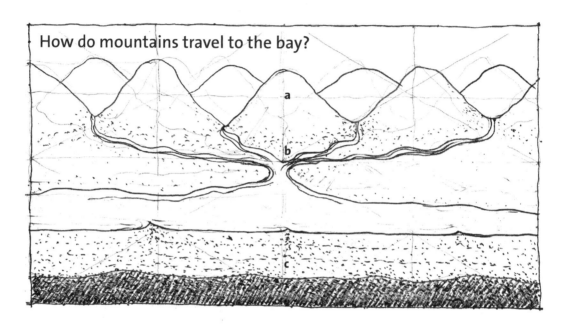

How do mountains travel to the bay?

a. slope: the inclined surface between the ridge line of a mountain range and its base.

b. river: a significant stream of water that travels through a natural channel from high to low ground.

c. sediment: small particles of rock and soil transported by water and gravity.

42 Erosion

The rivers and streams that run down the western slope of the Sierra Nevada are carrying the mountains to the bay.

As mountains weather, their stony surfaces slowly disintegrate into small particles of minerals and soil. Flowing water has energy, and streams moving down the Sierra's steep hillsides gain enough momentum to pick up loose bits of land. As the streams merge into rivers, water carries this sediment through the Central Valley, the California Delta, and the Carquinez Strait. Beyond the strait, the rivers spread out into San Francisco Bay. The water slows down. It loses energy, and the particles it holds fall to the bay's floor. The process of erosion – the removal of land – becomes deposition – the accretion of land.

Though it no longer flows in a straight line, water continues to move across the bay. Waves and tides lift the sediment that the rivers have deposited and put it back down in a new place. As they drift, these tiny pieces of land cloud the water. Turbidity is the measure of its cloudiness.

In the second half of the nineteenth century, miners in search of gold used water cannons to wash away hillsides in the Sierra. So much suspended land traveled downstream that the rivers were choked and a plume of gravel was carried miles beyond the Golden Gate. The bay floor changed forever.

Keywords: Physics, Souvenir, Water

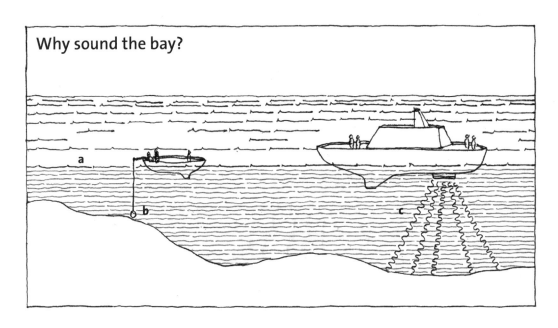

Why sound the bay?

a. sea level: the average elevation of the ocean's surface. The Coast Survey measures the depth of the seafloor in relation to low tide.

b. lead line: a rope with a lead weight at one end and markings of distance along its length.

c. SONAR: the acronym for sound navigation and ranging. SONAR instruments calculate depth through the emission of sound waves and the measurement of their travel time to the ocean floor and back.

43 Sounding

The depth of San Francisco Bay varies. Bedrock pokes through the mud of the bay floor. The tides that ebb and flow through the Golden Gate scour a deep channel at the strait and deposit sand in underwater dunes. Currents lift and drop sediment that piles up in shoals or drifts away from depressions. People have changed the bay's depth radically: hydraulic mining washed vast quantities of gravel and sediment from the Sierra onto the bay floor; the construction of new land made shoals and shallows higher; and blasting reduced the heights of rocks above and below the surface of the water. The ongoing dredging of the ship channel means moving sediment around the bay floor. The channel gets deeper, and other areas become shallower.

Charting the bottom of the bay is an economic necessity. Ships ply the bay constantly, and the hazards of unknown, uneven conditions below the surface of the water increase as vessel sizes grow. Founded to keep mariners safe, the US Office of Coast Survey has been measuring and mapping the contours of San Francisco Bay since 1850. Its early surveyors used direct means to calculate depths: they lowered sounding poles and lead lines to the bottom of the bay and then read depth marks one by one. Today, surveyors send an acoustic signal from their boats to the bay floor. They use time to measure space: counting the length of a sound's trip to the bottom and back in minutes and seconds lets them calculate its length in feet and inches.

Keywords: Interval, Navigation

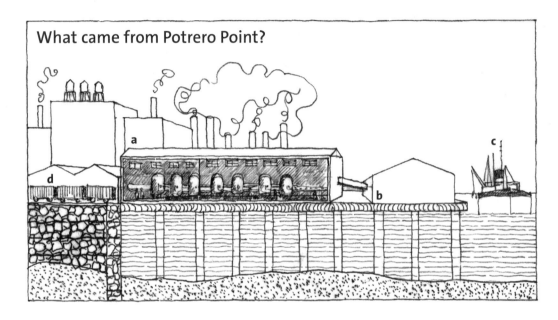

What came from Potrero Point?

a. factory: a building where machines and workers transform raw materials into manufactured goods.

b. warehouse: a building where raw materials or manufactured goods are stored between processing and distribution.

c. cargo ship: a seafaring vessel that carries raw materials from source to factory and finished goods from factory to market.

d. freight train: linked rail cars that carry raw materials and finished goods overland.

44 Potrero Point

Like an engine hidden behind the shiny surface of a machine, Potrero Point was the industrial center of San Francisco. Twenty years after the Gold Rush, factories had replaced pastures on the long ridge that extended east from Potrero Hill. The ridge itself was transformed in the service of industry: two square miles were broken down into rock to fill new land at the shore. From 1866 to 1868, between the establishment of the Pacific Rolling Mills and its production of the first finished iron on the west coast, hundreds of acres of ground were constructed and covered with foundries, storehouses, piers, and wharves. Land at Potrero Point was cheap; it was close enough to the city to be convenient but far enough to keep industrial nuisances out of the way; and its access to deep water offered easy berths for cargo ships. The point's factories produced iron, steel, sugar, ships, rope, barrels, mining equipment, and power. Its shipyards sustained the navy through two world wars; its manufacturers supplied the material – and a significant portion of the wealth – that built downtown San Francisco; and its mills rolled the tubes through which BART crosses San Francisco Bay.

Even though the economics of offshore manufacturing shuttered many of Potrero Point's factories, ships are still repaired there, and its generating station supplies a third of San Francisco's power. Part working landscape, part ghost town, and just a few minutes' drive from the extravagant pleasures of the northern waterfront, the point and its decaying industrial monuments are vestiges of a time when San Francisco was a workers' city.*

Keywords: Land, Work

---

* The industrial buildings in this drawing are based on the 1930 photograph "Western Sugar Refinery" on the website of the San Francisco Public Library.

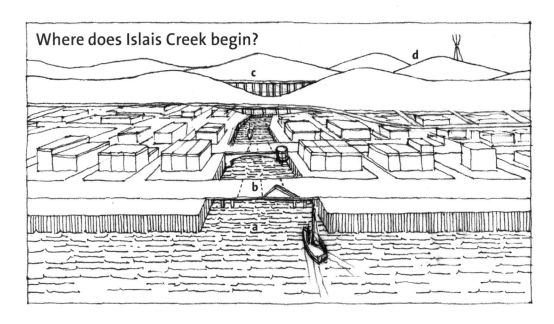

Where does Islais Creek begin?

a. channel: an engineered waterway built through wetlands or along the course of a stream.
b. drawbridge: a bridge that can be opened to permit boat traffic.
c. viaduct: the structure that carries a road over a wide valley.
d. headwaters: the beginning of a creek; the point farthest from its arrival at open water.

45 Islais Creek

Islais Creek Channel is the end of a line that connects San Francisco's edge to its center. That line – Islais Creek – has two branches. One, entirely hidden in pipes, begins on the north slope of San Bruno Mountain and runs below upper Alemany Boulevard. The other emerges on the east side of Mount Davidson, crosses the surface of Glen Canyon Park, and disappears into the city's storm sewer system. The tributaries meet underground near the Glen Park BART station, and the creek follows Alemany down toward San Francisco Bay (or rather, Alemany follows the creek, whose winding valley offered an easy route from the shore to the hills).

Islais Creek was buried during the construction of Alemany Boulevard, and the marsh and cove where it met San Francisco Bay were filled in to make new land. Out of sight and out of mind, it empties into Islais Creek Channel without sign or ceremony. But the view from the channel offers signs of vanished water. To the southwest, the highway bridge between Bernal Heights and the base of Mount Saint Joseph crosses the low land where Islais Creek used to spread into salt marsh; to the west, the bridge from Potrero Hill to Bernal Heights spans the old channel of Precita Creek, another buried stream. Topography tells a story. The same hills and valleys that turn the roadway into bridges once shaped the course of the creeks.

Keywords: Souvenir, Water

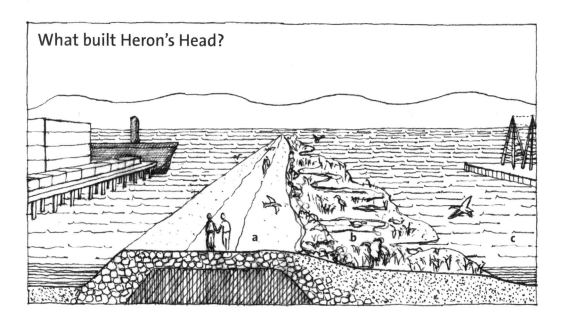

What built Heron's Head?

a. embankment: a linear platform of earth, clay, and stone built to carry a road through water or marshy ground.

b. marsh: low, saturated land that supports herbaceous plants. Coastal marshes emerge on the quiet sides of spits and jetties, where water deposits sand and sediment.

c. longshore drift: the transport of sand and sediment by waves breaking at an oblique angle to the coast. As a wave breaks, it carries sediment in its direction of travel; as it retreats, gravity makes the sediment fall onto the shore. With each advance and retreat, the sediment is carried farther down the coast.

46 Heron's Head

The combined product of intention and accident, Heron's Head Park exists because abandoned infrastructure became an armature for new nature.

In 1970, the Port of San Francisco began to build new land at India Basin. The project, Pier 98, was to serve two ends: to house a terminal for container ships and to provide the western anchorage for a new bridge across the bay. After seven years of construction, work stopped. The proposal for a southern bay crossing had been defeated in a referendum, and the container port at Oakland had grown so large that San Francisco couldn't compete.

For years the forsaken embankment was subject only to the action of waves and tides. Longshore drift deposited sediment and sand on the jetty's southern side. Plants and animals colonized the new land, and a marsh emerged from the rubble. A legal settlement, restitution for the port's use of substandard fill, turned the accidental landscape into a wetland garden. The agency was required to remove thousands of tons of concrete, asphalt, and debris; to dig a channel that let water flow into tidal and intertidal ponds; and to help environmental groups encourage flora and fauna. In 1999, Pier 98 became a park, named for its aerial resemblance to one of the blue herons that had found a home there. The reconstruction of the shore's edge for industry had led to the re-creation of a vanished ecology.

Keywords: Infrastructure, Interval, Physics, Play, Water

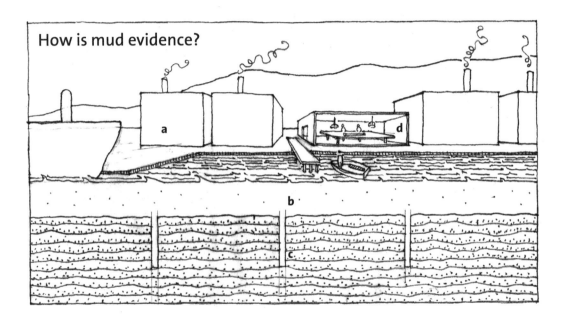

How is mud evidence?

a. factories: buildings in which raw materials are processed and goods are made.

b. sediment: small particles of silt and soil transported by water and gravity.

c. core sample: a cylindrical section of the material that comprises the bay floor.

d. laboratory: a space whose controlled conditions allow the precise measurement and analysis of physical and chemical compounds.

47 Mud

The floor of San Francisco Bay is a *corpus delicti*, evidence of industrial pollution. Like the television detective Columbo, soil scientists and chemists called to the scene of the crime begin with a body, a column of mud extracted from the sediment at the bottom of the bay. Frozen and dissected, the core discloses not only the poisons in the mud but also the chronology of wrongdoing: because contaminants are deposited in layers of sediment, depth acts as a measure of time. Data from the forensic analysis of the core answer the questions *what?* and *when?* Correlated with the records of nearby factories, they become essential clues to *who?* and *where? Why?* is known. Industry at the edge of the bay created wealth, built cities, and defended the nation. Its ecological consequences only emerged after the fact.

In 1980, after a series of environmental catastrophes across the United States, Congress passed the Comprehensive Environmental Response, Compensation, and Liability Act to redress the public hazard of abandoned industrial waste. The act, known informally as Superfund, provided criteria for identifying toxic sites, established protocols for tracing contaminants to their sources, and held contaminators liable for the cost of cleanup. The intersection of ecology with the legal system put a price tag on pollution, turned mud into state's evidence, and prompted investigations that revealed the toxic side effects of more than one heroic endeavor. Hunters Point Naval Shipyard kept the Pacific fleet in shape to fight the Second World War, but it poisoned the shore. Yesterday's gain brought today's loss.

Keywords: Chemistry, Defense, Interval

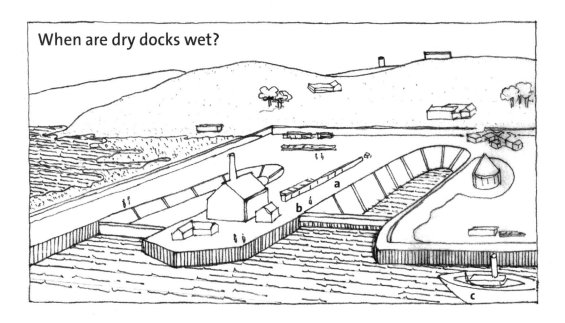

When are dry docks wet?

a. basis: a ship-shaped space at the edge of the harbor. Dry dock basins can be filled with water to float vessels in and out or pumped dry to allow their construction and repair.
b. gate: a watertight barrier that is opened to fill the basin and closed to empty it.
c. ship: a large vessel that navigates deep waters and long distances.

48 Dry Docks

Dry docks negotiate a maritime paradox: ships belong at sea, but they have to be built and maintained on land.

Long, narrow basins built into the shoreline, dry docks read as both fingers of the bay and extensions of the city. A ship in need of repair floats into a dry dock when its gates are open. The gates close, the water is pumped out, and shipbuilders go to work on the vessel, now balanced on dry ground. When the repair is finished – or when a new ship assembled in the dry dock is ready to embark – the gates are opened, water fills the space again, and the ship sails into the harbor.

The first permanent dry dock on the Pacific coast was built in 1868 at Hunters Point, the deepest stretch of San Francisco's shoreline. Forty years later, Roosevelt's Great White Fleet docked at the Hunters Point shipyard for repairs and demonstrated its strategic value to the military. The US Navy bought the shipyard in 1939, on the eve of the Second World War, and took possession eleven days after the bombing of Pearl Harbor. Over the course of the war, the navy expanded the shipyard by nearly six hundred acres and built four new dry docks. One of them was large enough to hold an aircraft carrier. From 1944 to 1965, the Hunters Point Naval Shipyard published its own newspaper: *The Drydocker.**

Keywords: Defense, Navigation, Work

---

* This drawing is based on two photographs, "Hunter's Point graving docks in the 1920s," on the website *Found SF*, and "Aerial view of Hunters Point Naval Shipyard with Dry Dock No. 4 in center, looking southwest," on the website of the Library of Congress.

Afterword

Observing: A Manifesto

Bay Lexicon is a manifesto, an argument that the observation, documentation, and discussion of landscapes as we find them are necessary steps toward informed public decisions about the future. The edge of San Francisco Bay is not unique. Inflected by the particulars of local geography, culture, institutions, and mythologies, negotiations between people and a dynamic environment shape every urban landscape. The climate emergency means that cities all over the world will need to revisit current compromises, and the reprises should use language that does justice to the complexity of the places they address.

Building vocabulary for the hybrid conditions of the Anthropocene requires more than the compilation of a list of words. Like Roget's original (unalphabetic) *Thesaurus*, it has to make "diagrams [of] the relationships of our words to our ideas, habits, and shared perceptions."[1] Illuminating the complex (and often invisible) interactions between natural forces and cultural intentions is recursive work. It needs to alternate between observation and reflection. It requires the examination and reclassification of the same information in light of plural ideas and perspectives. It must respect and make room for the different meanings that emerge when a landscape is seen through different lenses.

Landscapes are never fixed or final. They change as material artifacts and in our perceptions and desires. Language changes, too, and no lexicon has the last word. But every landscape lexicon comprises a portrait of its time and place: it represents the living engagement among words, speakers, and the world they inhabit, describe, and imagine.[2] And because the language we use to articulate our understanding of the present becomes the language we use to dream about the future, our landscape lexicons constitute frameworks for conversations and choices about values, uses, and forms. They set the terms for change.

---

1 Shattuck, "The Alphabet and the Junkyard," 35.
2 For a discussion of the dynamic character of dictionaries, see Mugglestone, *Dictionaries*, 16.

Acknowledgments

I owe many people thanks for this book's realization. It began with an invitation from Peter Richards and Susan Schwartzenberg to spend the summer of 2007 as a visiting artist at the Exploratorium. Since then, Susan has been an interlocutor, champion, and inspiration: our collaboration turned sketches and ideas into an installation at the museum's Bay Observatory Gallery, a book proposal, and a manuscript. The Seed Fund of San Francisco generously supported this process, and along the way, conversations with Megan and Rick Prelinger, Matthew Booker, and our Bay Observatory colleagues transformed my understanding of San Francisco Bay and its meanings. Ken Botnick provided graphic design guidance for the field entries, and Jacob Mitchell carried out their digital production. Charles Birnbaum, Ellen Braae, Matthew Gandy, Christophe Girot, Kristina Hill, Kelly Shannon, and Henriette Steiner invited me to talk and write about work in progress. Andrea Kahn edited early, middle, and late drafts, and Katherine Whitney offered insight as the manuscript came together. At McGill-Queen's University Press, Richard Ratzlaff saw the book's possibilities, and Kathleen Fraser and Matthew Kudelka coached me through its production. At the University of Toronto, research assistants Emily Cheng, Michael Cook, and Karen May supported initial work with the Observatory; Joshua Bauman, Amelia Hartin, Aaron Hernandez, and Elise Hunchuck made it possible to finish the book. Michael Collins, Batya Grundland, and Anne Mucha saw me through an injury that had derailed my work. Christina Kramer gave me the right advice at the right time. And to Amir Gavriely: thank you for everything.

Sources

The information in this book is drawn from field research and primary and secondary source texts. The list that follows includes the range of documents and digital archives I consulted, even if they are not cited directly in the text.

Digital Archives

A Treasury of World's Fair Art and Architecture, University of Maryland
Alameda County Open Data
ArcGIS Online
California Open Data Portal
DataSF
David Rumsey Map Collection
Found SF
Golden Gate National Recreation Area Park Archives
Historic American Buildings Survey (Library of Congress Prints and Photographs Division)
Living New Deal
Marin County Open Data
National Archives
National Park Service
San Francisco Public Library

Books and Articles

"A Guide to Eating San Francisco Bay Fish and Shellfish Based on Mercury or PBSS." *OEHHA*, 4 November 2011. http://oehha.ca.gov/advis ories/san-francisco-bay.

Alexander, Christopher, Sara Isikawa, Murray Silverstein, et al. *A Pattern Language: Towns, Buildings, Construction*. Oxford: Oxford University Press, 1977.

"Aquatic Park Historic District." *National Park Service: Architecture in the Parks*. https://www. nps.gov/parkhistory/online_books/harrison/ harrison29.htm

Banham, Reyner. *Los Angeles: The Architecture of Four Ecologies*, 2nd ed. Berkeley: University of California Press, 2009.

Bartley, Eddie, Alan Hopkins, Noreen Weeden, and Matt Zlatunich. *A Field Guide to 100 Birds of Heron's Head: Islais Creek to Candlestick Point, San Francisco*. Edited by Mark Chambers. Bayview: NorCal Printing, 2010.

Bay Conservation and Development Commission. *Agreement for a Wetlands Enhancement and Creation and Passive Recreation Project by the Port of San Francisco at Pier 98 in India Basin along the Southern San Francisco Waterfront*. 1993.

Benedict, Burton. *The Anthropology of World's Fairs: San Francisco's Panama Pacific International Exposition of 1915*. Berkeley and London: Lowie Museum of Anthropology; Scolar Press, 1983.

Birt, Rodger C. *History's Anteroom: Photography of San Francisco 1906–1909*. Richmond: William Stout, 2011.

Black, Andy and Sam Green. *A Cinematic Study of Fog in San Francisco*. 2013.

Boas, Franz. *Handbook of American Indian Languages*. Washington: US GPO, 1911.

Booker, Matthew Morse. *Down by the Bay: San Francisco's History between the Tides*. Berkeley: University of California Press, 2013.

Brechin, Gray. *Imperial San Francisco: Urban Power, Earthly Ruin*. Berkeley: University of California Press, 1999.

Bright, William. *1500 California Place Names: Their Origin and Meaning*. Berkeley: University of California Press, 1998.

California Department of Fish and Wildlife. "2017–2018 California Commercial Herring Fishery

FAQ Sheet." https://nrm.dfg.ca.gov/FileHand
ler.ashx?DocumentID=151147&inline

– "Table 10 – Monthly Landings in Pounds in the
San Francisco Area During 2017." https://nrm.
dfg.ca.gov/FileHandler.ashx?DocumentID=15955
0&inline.

California State Coastal Conservancy and Ocean
Protection Council, NOAA National Marine
Fisheries Service and Restoration Center, San
Francisco Bay Conservation and Development
Commission, and San Francisco Estuary Part-
nership. "Chapter Eight: Submerged Aquatic
Vegetation." *San Francisco Bay Subtidal Habitat
Goals Report.* 2010.

"CEQA: The California Environmental Quality
Act." *California Natural Resources Agency.* https://
resources.ca.gov/ceqa.

Chin, John L., Florence L. Wong, and Paul R. Carl-
son. "Shifting Shoals and Shattered Rocks – How
Man Has Transformed the Floor of the West-
Central San Francisco Bay." USGS Circular 1259.
Reston: US Department of the Interior and US
Geological Survey, 2004. https://pubs.usgs.gov/
circ/2004/c1259/c1259.pdf.

Clauss, F.J. *Alcatraz: Island of Many Mistakes.*
Menlo Park: Briarcliff Press, 1981.

Cohen, Andrew. *An Introduction to the San Francisco Estuary.* 3rd ed. San Francisco: San Francisco Estuary Project; Save the Bay; San
Francisco Estuary Institute, 2000.

Cohen, Andrew N., and James T. Carlton. *Nonindigenous Aquatic Species in a United States Estuary: A Case Study of the Biological Invasions of the
San Francisco Bay and Delta.* Washington, DC:
US Fish and Wildlife Service, 1995.

Corbett, Michael R. *Port City: The History and
Transformation of the Port of San Francisco, 1848–
2010.* San Francisco: San Francisco Architectural
Heritage, 2010.

Cosco Busan Oil Spill Trustees. Cosco Busan *Oil
Spill Final Damage Assessment and Restoration
Plant/Environmental Assessment.* Prepared by
California Department of Fish and Game,
California State Lands Commission, National
Oceanic and Atmospheric Administration,
United States Fish and Wildlife Service, National
Park Service, Bureau of Land Management. 2012.

Crutzen, Paul J. "Geology of Mankind." *Nature* 415,
no. 6867 (2002): 23.

Csanady, G.T. *Air–Sea Interaction: Laws and Mechanisms.* Cambridge: Cambridge University Press,
2001.

Dartnell, Peter, Patrick Barnard, John L. Chin,
Daniel Hanes, Rikk G. Kvitek, Pat J. Impietro,
and James V. Gardner. "Under the Golden Gate
Bridge – Views of the Sea Floor near the Entrance to San Francisco Bay, California." USGS,
7 July 2006. https://pubs.usgs.gov/sim/2006/
2917/sim2917.pdf.

Delgado, James P. *Adventures of a Sea Hunter.* V
ancouver: Douglas and McIntyre, 2004.

– *Alcatraz: Island of Change.* Golden Gate National
Recreation Area. San Francisco: Golden Gate
National Park Association, 1991.

– "A Dream of Seven Decades: San Francisco's
Aquatic Park." *California History* 64, no. 4 (1985):
272–82.

– *Gold Rush Port: The Maritime Archaeology of San
Francisco's Waterfront.* Berkeley: University of
California Press, 2009.

DeNardo, T.A., ed. "Collision under the Golden
Gate." US Coast Guard Department of Transportation. *Proceedings of the Marine Safety Council*
28, no. 11 (1971): 201–210.

Devitt, Elizabeth. "Explaining the Cosco Busan
Spill's Toxic Effects: Scientists Report a Link
between Oil and Fish Heart Health." *Bay Nature,*
9 April 2014.

Dow, Gerald Robert. "Bay Fill in San Francisco: A
History of Change." Master's thesis, California
State University, 1973.

Elder, William P. "Geology of the Golden Gate
Headlands." In *Geology and Natural History of
the San Francisco Bay Area: A Field-Trip Guide-
book,* edited by Philip W. Stoffer and Leslie C.
Gordon, 61–86. *US Geological Survey Bulletin*
no. 2188, 2001.

Ellsworth, W.L. "The Great 1906 San Francisco
Earthquake." USGS. http://earthquake.usgs.gov/
regional/nca/1906/18april/index.php.

Elms, Alan C. "Apocryphal Freud: Sigmund
Freud's Most Famous 'Quotations' and Their
Actual Sources." *The Annual of Psychoanalysis*
29 (2001): 83–104.

Embley, Bob. "Seafloor Mapping." *NOAA Ocean Explorer*. https://oceanexplorer.noaa.gov/explorations/02fire/background/seafloor_mapping/seafloor.html.

Fardon, George Robinson. *San Francisco Album: Photographs of the Most Beautiful Views and Public Buildings*. San Francisco: Fraenkel Gallery, 1999.

Faulkner, William. *Requiem for a Nun*. New York: Vintage Books, 2011.

Finch, Kelsey. "Trouble in Paradise: Postwar History of San Francisco's Hunters Point." Honors thesis, Stanford University, 2008. https://files-urbanstudies-stanford-edu.s3.amazonaws.com/s3fs-public/kfinch_honorsthesis_compressed.pdf.

Gilliam, Harold. *Weather of the San Francisco Bay Region*. Berkeley: University of California Press, 2002.

Goudie, Andrew, and Heather Viles. *Landscapes and Geomorphology: A Very Short Introduction*. Oxford: Oxford University Press, 2010.

Hanson, Warren D. *San Francisco Water and Power: A History of the Municipal Water Department and Hetch Hetchy System*. 3rd ed. San Francisco: City and County of San Francisco, 1994.

Harrison, Stephan, Steve Pile, and Nigel Thrift, eds. *Patterned Ground: Entanglements of Nature and Culture*. London: Reaktion Books, 2004.

Hayes, Anne. *Finding Urban Nature: An Educator's Guide to Exploring San Francisco Natural History*. San Francisco: The Crissy Field Center, 2010.

Hayes, Derek. *Historical Atlas of California*. Berkeley: University of California Press, 2007.

Heyes, Scott A. "Between the Trees and the Tides: Inuit Ways of Discriminating Space in a Coastal and Boreal Landscape." In *Landscape in Language: Transdisciplinary Perspectives*, edited by David M. Mark et al., 187–224. Amsterdam and Philadelphia: John Benjamins, 2011.

"Hunters Point Naval Shipyard." *United States Environmental Protection Agency*. 22 February 2017. https://yosemite.epa.gov/r9/sfund/r9sfdocw.nsf/vwsoalphabetic/hunters+point+naval+shipyard?opendocument.

Incardona, J.P., C.A. Vines, B.F. Anulacion, D.H. Baldwin, H.L. Day, B.L. French, J.S. Labenia, et al. "Unexpectedly High Mortality in Pacific Herring Embryos Exposed to the 2007 *Cosco Busan* Oil Spill in San Francisco Bay." *Proceedings of the National Academy of Sciences* 109, no. 2 (2012). https://doi.org/10.1073/pnas.1108884109.

International Bird Rescue. "Cosco Busan Bird Toll Update; Plovers Survive Spill." *International Bird Rescue*, 26 January 2010.

Jackson, Eric P. "The Early Historical Geography of San Francisco." *The Journal of Geography* 26, no. 1 (January 1927): 12–22.

Knockelman, William J., T. John Conomos, and Alan E. Leviton, eds. *San Francisco Bay: Use and Protection*. San Francisco: California Academy of Sciences, Pacific Division of the American Association for the Advancement of Science, 1982.

Lacerda, Luiz D., and Wim Salomons, "The Use of Mercury Amalgamation in Gold and Silver Mining." In *Mercury from Gold and Silver Mining: A Chemical Time Bomb?*, 1–3. Berlin and New York: Springer, 1998.

Lopez, Barry, and Debra Gwartney, eds. *Home Ground: A Guide to the American Landscape*. San Antonio: Trinity University Press, 2013.

Macfarlane, Robert. *Landmarks*. London: Hamish Hamilton, 2015.

Macfarlane, Robert, and Jackie Morris. *The Lost Words*. Toronto: House of Anansi Press, 2018.

"Major Oil Spills and Incidents in California." Office of Spill Prevention and Response, 20 February 2013.

Martini, John A. *Fort Point: Sentry at the Golden Gate*. Golden Gate National Recreation Area. San Francisco: Golden Gate National Park Association, 1991.

Mathur, Anuradha, and Dilip da Cunha. "Wetness Is Everywhere." *Journal of Architectural Education* 74, no. 1 (2020): 139–140.

McHarg, Ian L. *Design with Nature*. Garden City: Natural History Press, 1969.

Mensch, E. Cromwell. *San Francisco Oakland Bay Bridge: A Technical Description in Ordinary Language*. San Francisco: [self-published], 1936.

"Mercury." *USGS* California Water Science Center, 23 December 2016. https://ca.water.usgs.gov/mercury.

Molnar, Jennifer L., Rebecca L. Gamboa, Carmen

Revenga, and Mark D. Spalding. "Assessing the Global Threat of Invasive Species to Marine Biodiversity." *Frontiers in Ecology and the Environment* 6, no. 9 (2008): 485–492.

Monroe, Michael, and Judy Kelly. *State of the Estuary: A Report on Conditions and Problems in the San Francisco Bay/San Joaquin Delta Estuary.* Oakland: San Francisco Estuary Project. Prepared in cooperation with the US Environmental Protection Agency by the Association of Bay Area Governments, 1992.

Morrish, William Rees. *Civilizing Terrains: Mountains, Mounds and Mesas.* San Francisco: William Stout Publishers, 1996.

Mugglestone, Lynda. *Dictionaries: A Very Short Introduction.* Oxford: Oxford University Press, 2011.

Muir, John. "The Hetch Hetchy Valley." *Weekly Transcript* (Boston), 25 March 1873.

– *The Yosemite.* New York: The Century Company, 1912.

Myrick, David F. *San Francisco's Telegraph Hill.* Berkeley: Howell North, 1972.

National Environmental Policy Act. nepa.gov. https://ceq.doe.gov/index.html.

National Transportation Safety Board. "Allision of Hong Kong–Registered Containership M/V *Cosco Busan* with the Delta Tower of the San Francisco–Oakland Bay Bridge, San Francisco, California, November 7, 2007." Marine Accident Report NTSB/MAR-09/01. Washington, DC: National Transportation Safety Board, 2009. https://www.ntsb.gov/investigations/Accident Reports/Reports/MAR0901.pdf.

– "Marine Casualty Report: Collision Involving the SS *Arizona Standard* and SS *Oregon Standard* at the Entrance to San Francisco Bay on January 18, 1971." Washington, DC: Department of Transportation, 1 August 1971. https://www.uscg.mil/hq/cg5/cg545/docs/boards/arizonoregon.pdf.

"New Almaden Mining Historic District California." National Park Service. https://www.nps.gov/nr/travel/american_latino_heritage/new_almaden_mining_historic_district.html.

Office of the City Administrator, Office of Resilience and Capital Planning. *Fortifying San Francisco's Great Seawall: Strategies for Funding the Seawall Resiliency Project.* San Francisco: City and County of San Francisco, June 2017. http://onesanfrancisco.org/sites/default/files/inline-files/Seawall%20Finance%20Work%20Group%20Report%20Final%20version.pdf.

Okamoto, Ariel Rubissow, and Kathleen M. Wong. *Natural History of San Francisco Bay.* Berkeley: University of California Press, 2011.

Oppenheimer, Frank. "Rationale for a Science Museum." *Curator: The Museum Journal* 11, no. 3 (September 1968): 206–9.

Peterson, David H., et al. "Seasonal/Yearly Salinity Variations in San Francisco Bay." USGS, 13 December 2007. https://sfbay.wr.usgs.gov/hydroclimate/sal_variations.

Ricketts, Edward F., and Jack Calvin. *Between Pacific Tides: An Account of the Habits and Habitats of Some Five Hundred of the Common, Conspicuous Seashore Invertebrates of the Pacific Coast Between Sitka, Alaska, and Northern Mexico.* Redwood City: Stanford University Press, 1939.

Rothman, Hal K. *The Park That Makes Its Own Weather: An Administrative History of the Golden Gate National Recreation Area.* San Francisco: Golden Gate National Recreation Area, 2002.

Rubin, Jasper. *A Negotiated Landscape: The Transformation of San Francisco's Waterfront since 1950.* Chicago: Center for American Places at Columbia College Chicago, 2011.

San Francisco Department of City Planning. 1948. *Progress in City Planning. A Report to the People of San Francisco.* 1948. http://archive.org/details/SanFranciscoDepartmentOfCityPlanning1948ProgressInCityPlanning.

Schweikart, Larry, and Lynne Pierson-Doti, "From Hard Money to Branch Banking: California Banking in the Gold Rush Economy." In *A Golden State: Mining and Economic Development in Gold Rush California*, edited by James R. Rawls and Richard J. Orsi, 209–232. Berkeley: University of California Press, 1999.

"Sea Level Rise Viewer." NOAA *Office for Coastal Management*, July 2019. https://coast.noaa.gov/slr.

Sharpsteen, William Crittenden. "Vanished Waters of Southeastern San Francisco: Notes on Mission Bay and the Marshes and Creeks of the Potreros and the Bernal Rancho." *California Historical Society Quarterly* 21, no. 2 (1942): 113–126.

Shattuck, Roger. "The Alphabet and the Junkyard." In *The Innocent Eye*, 32–39. Boston: MFA, 2003.

Shin, Eung-Bai, and Peter Krenkel. "Mercury Uptake by Fish and Biomethylation Mechanisms." *Journal (Water Pollution Control Federation)* 48, no. 3, pt. I (March 1976): 473–501.

Simone, Nina. *Black Gold.* Stroud Productions, RCA Victor. 1970.

Simons, Eric. "The San Francisco Bay Is Wild Still." *Bay Nature,* 1 January 2017.

Sloan, Doris, and John A. Karachewski. *Geology of the San Francisco Bay Region.* Berkeley: University of California Press, 2006.

Smith, Susan E. and Susumu Kato. "The Fisheries of San Francisco Bay: Past, Present, and Future." In *San Francisco Bay: The Urbanized Estuary: Investigations into the Natural History of San Francisco Bay and Delta with Reference to the Influence of Man: Fifty-Eighth Annual Meeting of the Pacific Division/American Association for the Advancement of Science held at the San Francisco State University, San Francisco, California, June 12–16, 1977,* edited by T. John Conomos, Alan E. Leviton, and Margaret Berson, 445–68. San Francisco: The Division, 1979.

Solnit, Rebecca. *Infinite City: A San Francisco Atlas.* Berkeley: University of California Press, 2010.

Sommer, Lauren. "San Francisco Is Fighting California's Plan to Save Salmon. Wait. What?" *NPR,* 22 May 2011.

Spirn, Anne Whiston. *The Granite Garden: Urban Nature and Human Design.* New York: Basic Books, 1989.

– "Landscape Literacy and Design for Ecological Democracy: The Nature of Mill Creek, West Philadelphia." In *Grounding Urban Natures: Histories and Futures of Urban Ecologies,* edited by Henrik Ernstson and Sverker Sörlin, 109–136. Cambridge, MA: MIT Press, 2019.

– *The Language of Landscape.* New Haven: Yale University Press, 1998.

Stilgoe, John R. *Shallow Water Dictionary: A Grounding in Estuary English.* New York: Princeton Architectural Press, 2004.

– *What Is Landscape?* Cambridge, MA: MIT Press, 2018.

"Subtidal Habitat Goals Report." San Francisco Bay Subtidal Habitat Goals Project: Conservation Planning for the Submerged Areas of the Bay, 2010. http://www.sfbaysubtidal.org/report.html.

"Superfund." *US Environmental Protection Agency,* 22 May 2017. https://www.epa.gov/superfund.

"Swamp and Overflow Lands." California State Lands Commission. 2015. http://www.slc.ca.gov/Info/Swamp_Overflow.html.

Thompson, Edwin N., and Sally B. Woodbridge. *Presidio of San Francisco: An Outline of Its Evolution as a US Army Post, 1847–1990.* US Department of the Interior, 1992. Digitized by the Internet Archive, 2007. https://archive.org/details/presidioofsanfra00deparich.

US Coast Survey. *The City of San Francisco and its Vicinity* [map]. 1:10000. Washington, 1852.

– *City of San Francisco and Its Vicinity, California* [map]. 1:10,000. 61x89 cm. Washington, 1859.

– *Entrance to San Francisco Bay California* [map]. 1:50,000. Washington, 1859.

US Department of Commerce, National Oceanic and Atmospheric Administration. "What Causes Ocean Currents?" *Ocean Explorer,* 14 February 2013. http://oceanexplorer.noaa.gov/facts/currents.html.

US Department of the Interior, Bureau of Land Management. "California Coastal National Monument, Draft Resource Management Plan/Draft Environmental Impact Statement" 2005.

US Department of the Interior and US Geological Survey. "Continuous Monitoring of Water Quality and Suspended-Sediment Transport in the San Francisco Bay and Delta." USGS, 3 January 2017. https://ca.water.usgs.gov/projects/baydelta.

US EPA (Environmental Protection Agency). "Treasure Island Naval Station-Hunters Point Annex, San Francisco, CA: Cleanup Progress." https://cumulis.epa.gov/supercpad/Site Profiles/index.cfm?fuseaction=second.schedule&id=0902722.

University of Rhode Island and Inner Space Center. "How Fast Does Sound Travel?" *Discovery of Sound in the Sea.*

Upton, M.G. "The Plan of San Francisco." *The Overland Monthly* 2 (1869): 131–36. http://urbanplanning.library.cornell.edu/DOCS/upton.htm.

Vance, James. *Geography and Urban Evolution in the San Francisco Bay Area*. Berkeley: University of California Institute of Governmental Studies, 1964.

Veronico, Betty S. *Images of America: Lighthouses of the Bay Area*. Charleston: Arcadia, 2008.

Virtual Tour San Francisco Maritime National Historic Park. "A Signal Station of Telegraph Hill: Gold Rush Communications." National Park Service. https://www.nps.gov/features/safr/feat0001/virtualships/vrmovies/muvr2hs5.htm.

White, Richard. *The Organic Machine: The Remaking of the Columbia River*. New York: Hill and Wang, 1996.

Whiting, Sam. "When the Foghorns Blow." S F *Gate*, 6 July 2009.

Whorf, Benjamin Lee. "Science and Linguistics" [1940]. In *The Routledge Language and Cultural Theory Reader*, edited by Lucy Burke, Tony Crowley, and Alan Girvin, 114–21. London and New York: Routledge, 2001.

Williamson, R.S., and W.H. Heuer. *Report Upon the Removal of Blossom Rock in San Francisco Harbor, California*. Washington: US GPO, 1871. https://archive.org/details/ReportUponThe RemovalOfBlossomRockInSanFrancisco Harbor.

Wolff, Jane. "Bay Lexicon." Installation. Ongoing beginning 2013, The Exploratorium (Bay Observatory Gallery), San Francisco, as part of the museum's permanent collection.

– "*Bay Lexicon*: Vocabulary as Manifesto." San Francisco: The Exploratorium, 2015.

– "City, Nature, Infrastructure: A Brief Lexicon." In *Routledge Research Companion to Landscape Architecture*, edited by Ellen Braae and Henriette Steiner, 193–202. New York: Routledge, 2019.

– "Lexicon as Theory: Some Definitions at the Edge of San Francisco Bay." In *Delta Dialogues*, edited by Christophe Girot, Susann Ahn, Isabelle Fehlmann, and Lara Mehling, 14–24. Zürich: ETH Zürich, 2017.

Ziccardi, Mike. "Cosco-Busan Oil Spill." *Oiled Wildlife Care Network*, 7 November 2012.

Index

Great White Fleet, 15, 33, 117, 165
Green, Sam, 73n
Green Street (San Francisco), 119, 122–3
Greenwich stairs, 121
Griffin, Taylor, 35
groundwater, 90, 108
Gwartney, Debra, 5n4

habitat, 27–30, 104; and salinity, 108
Half Moon Bay, 147
Harding Rock, 151
Harrison, Stephan, 5n4
hazards, to navigation, 72, 73, 113
headwaters, 158
herons, 161
Heron's Head, 23, 24, 28, 45, 48, 54–5, 58, 59, 68–9, 160–1
Heron's Head Park, 161
herring, 147
Hetch Hetchy Aqueduct, 25, 47–8
Hetch Hetchy Dam, 19, 25, 47, 93
Heyes, Scott, 3n1
Hoffer, Eric, 50
Holloran, Peter, 47n7
Home Ground: A Guide to the American Landscape (Lopez and Gwartney), 5n4
houseboats, 55, 68, 150–1
Houston, flooding in, 4
hull, 88
Hunters Point, 26–7, 33–4, 83, 147; dry dock, 165
Hunters Point Naval Shipyard, 33, 58, 163, 165

Ice Age, 17, 48, 62, 101, 139
India Basin, 161
Indian Ocean, 77
infrastructure (keyword), 45–8; bar and harbor pilots, 79; bridge, 141; cracks, 111; Embarcadero, 129; foghorns, 73; seawall, 83; tap, 93; terrace, 119; tides, 75
interface, 104, 114

interference, 104
interior, 70
International Longshoreman's and Warehousemen's Union, 50
interruption, 114
intersections, 67, 98–9
interval (keyword), 57–61; Aquatic Park, 103; bridge, 141; collision, 147; Doyle Drive, 81; Embarcadero, 129; Heron's Head, 161; Mission Rock, 151; mud, 163; Palace of Fine Arts, 85; piers, 105; salinity, 109; sounding, 155; tides, 75; tunnel, 127
Islais Creek, 20, 62, 68–9, 158–9
Islais Creek Channel, 159
islands, 17–18, 67, 100–1; and shoals, 138–9
isolation, 101

jetty, 102
Jones Street (San Francisco), 126

Katrina, Hurricane, 4
keel, 88

laboratory, 162
lagoon, 84
land (keyword), 14–17; cliff, 123; cracks, 111; filled, 82, 83, 84, 148; Fort Mason, 97; Fort Point, 71; ground, 90; houseboats, 149; Mission Rock, 151; Potrero Point, 157; seawall, 83; shoals, 139; tall buildings, 131; Telegraph Hill, 117; underground, 130; vertical, 130–1
landing, 86
landmark, 86
Landmarks (MacFarlane), 5n4
landscapes, vocabulary for describing, 3–10
Landscapes and Geomorphology: A Very Short Introduction (Goudie and Viles), 61n7
Lands End, 73

language: and culture, 3–4; vocabulary for describing landscapes, 3–10
Language of Landscape, The (Spirn), 5n4
Larkin Street (San Francisco), 127
lead line, 154
Leavenworth Street (San Francisco), 30
lexicon, as tool, 11
light, 22; wrecks, 67, 114–15
lighthouses, 89
Linnaeus, Carl, 27
Living New Deal, The (website), 103n
Lloyd, Carol, 55n12
Loma Prieta earthquake (1989), 32, 60, 61, 129
Lombard Street (San Francisco), 81
Long Bridge, 149
longshore drift, 18, 160, 161
Lopez, Barry, 5n4
Los Angeles, 26
Los Angeles: The Architecture of Four Ecologies (Banham), 61n7
Lost Words, The (McFarlane and Morris), 5n4

Macor, Michael, 147
maintain, 111
maps, land and water on, 14
marina, 55–6, 67, 86–7
Marina District, 60, 83, 87
Marina Green, 44, 67, 91
Marin County, 81, 101
Maritime Museum, 103
Market Street (San Francisco), 133
marsh, 24, 160, 161
Mason Street (San Francisco), 126, 127
mast, 88
Mathur, Anuradha, 14n2
matter, 22
McCarthy, Joseph, 11n8
McFarlane, Robert, 5n4